ANTONI GAUDÍ

© 2009 EVERGREEN GmbH, Köln

Publisher: Paco Asensio
Authors: Aurora Cuito, Cristina Montes
Editorial coordination: Simone K. Schleifer
Editor: Mariana R. Eguaras Etchetto
English translation: Juliet King
German translation: Bettina Beck
Revision of the English translation:
Michael Scuffil
Revision of the German translation:
Ricarda Essrich

Art director: Mireia Casanovas Soley
Graphic design and layout: Anabel Naranjo
Cover design: Catinka Keul

Cover photo: Casa Batlló, roof
Copyright © Paul Raftery / VIEW

ISBN 978-3-8365-1165-0

Printed in China

ANTONI GAUDÍ

COMPLETE WORKS
SÄMTLICHE WERKE

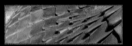

The Gaudí Phenomenon.
Nature, technique and artistry

Das Phänomen Gaudí.
Natur, Technik und Handwerk

The Gaudí Phenomenon

In light of the growing and general recognition of Gaudí's work, more than 150 years after his birth, I ponder the reason for this phenomenon, which is so unusual in the field of architecture. Gaudí did not become a success as a result of the quantity of works completed, since he only directed about 20 important projects. Nor is his success due to the wide geographic diffusion of his buildings, since the majority of them are concentrated in the city of Barcelona. Neither is the architect's fame due to the fact that he was a great promoter of his work and character, since he isolated himself from everything that could disturb his work. Nor were his proposals accepted with enthusiasm by his contemporaries who, in general, were hostile towards them. Therefore, we see that it is not easy to find reasonable answers that justify Gaudí's current fame, nor the indifference that he was subjected to right up to his death in 1926.

Gaudí's secret was probably knowing how to tackle architectural creation in a distinct manner, without artistic or technical prejudices. His knowledge of the trades and the procedures of construction permitted him to stand out in his era. He practiced an eclectic

rchitecture in agreement with the rules of the 19th century and the neo-Romantic and Baroque tastes of Modernism. Gaudí was as distinguished a figure as Domènech i Montaner or Puig i Cadafalch, in his most immediate context, or as V. Horta, H. Guimard, C. R. Mackintosh, O. Wagner, J. Hoffman or J. M. Olbrich, at the European level, all architects with grand personalities who formulated their own language and thus occupy important pages in the history of art and architecture. Nevertheless, Gaudí is something more. He is a virile and overwhelming individual, capable of breaking tradition, with fidelity to historic styles and the determination to please the euphoric bourgeoisie of the 1900s. He replanted the essence of architecture and reconsidered tastes and materials, procedures, techniques, systems of calculation, geometric repertoires, etc. It's not

that he wanted to start from scratch: by dominating the resources of architecture, whether stylistic or technical, he could embark on a personal adventure based on a playful intuition that allowed him to create works with independence and originality. No one can confirm that Gaudí was a visionary; even though there are people who dare to state it, basing their argument on a hypothetical esotericism of the system of symbols that he used. Gaudí was one of the most illustrious minds in the transition from the 19th to the 20th century. He perceived that it was necessary to end a certain neo-medieval Romanticism that proliferated in Europe during the era. The world was changing and it was necessary to put into place other systems of life, which architecture had to express.

Gaudí obtained the title of architect at Barcelona's

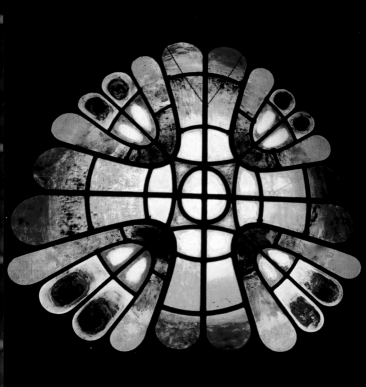

demanding Escuela Técnica Superior de Arquitectura in 1878. His studies, combined with his domination of the language and the materials of the artistic profession, which he learned alongside his father in Reus and at Barcelona's best workshops, led him to create his first projects by trial and error, with neo-Gothic and Arabic remembrances. His experiences culminated in the Casa Vicens in Barcelona, where he tackled a type of constructional solution that, today, we can confirm is the seed of an unmistakable vocabulary based on warped surfaces, paraboloids and hyperboloids, helical rhythms, and the use of a fiery polychrome. This vocabulary stood apart from any style of the past to obey an architecture without isms, an architecture that, as his disciple Martinell said, we can only call "Gaudíism."

In his maturity, Gaudí was inclined towards an empirical work

philosophy. This meant that he relied on experience and accepted those things which saw their best moments during the 18th century. The architect's propensity for everything tried-and-tested probably also came from the "common sense" of rural people from the Tarragona countryside. They are practical people, dedicated to work and to saving resources and energies. For one reason or another, Gaudí reached a point in his career when he put architectural procedures to the test. He transformed his workshops into laboratories, he worked with experimental models, and he searched for resistant materials (granite, basalt, porphyry, etc.). He proposed undulating walls and ceilings, he opted for oblique columns and was interested in the path of light and the ventilation of buildings. He calculated the structures of his properties with overhead power cable arches. He also used mirrors, photography and non-Euclidean geometry to design his volumes. His audacity surprised many and was understood by few, but resulted in such impressive designs as the crypt of the Colònia Güell, the Pedrera, Park Güell, and the Temple of the Sagrada Família. These works were easily criticized by the public and by certain members of the press, but their unusual force always astonished. Francesc Pujols, a popular philosopher of the era and a friend of Gaudí, stated that "in all the works of the great Gaudí, what happened was that no one liked them, nor was there anyone who dared to say it to his face, because he had a style that asserted itself without pleasing." This affirmation seems a little out of place today, since Gaudí's projects not only continue to provoke consternation; they have been transformed into cult objects by a majority of the world's citizens.

And here we discover Gaudí's survival. Some of his buildings have been declared World Heritage Sites by UNESCO. Most of them have been restored and rehabilitated, and in many cases, have gone from private to public ownership. During his lifetime, Gaudí said that Casa Milà, more widely known as the Pedrera, would end up as a big hotel or a congressional palace. His prediction came true in 1996 when a financial group transformed the building into a cultural center. And the Pedrera is not the only building that has changed uses: the coach-house pavilions on the Güell estate are today the headquarters of the Real Cátedra Gaudí, attached to the Universitat Politècnica de Catalunya. Palau Güell (residence of his patron), Park Güell, the Sagrada Família, and the crypt of the Colònia Güell are all open to the public. On the ground floor of the Casa Calvet, there is a restaurant that conserves the original property. Casa Batlló is a convention center that is partially open to the public and, as mentioned previously, the Pedrera is a cultural center that includes an exhibition hall, an auditorium, a period apartment and, in the attic and on the building's terrace roof, a space called Espai Gaudí. The Palacio episcopal de Astorga houses a museum and the Casa de los Botines in León contains the headquarters of a financial group and a permanent exhibition hall. Finally, El Capricho in Comillas now contains a restaurant.

These Gaudí buildings are open to the public thanks to their exceptional personality. Though each one of the works has metamorphosed, Gaudí remains in force. The best way that we could pay homage to the great architect and artist is to visit his buildings and to know his work. Only in this way can we understand the enormous coherence that exists between his constructional systems, his habitable spaces, and his façades and roofs. Because Gaudí is indivisible; because he is the logic of form and the exaltation of art.

Daniel Giralt-Miracle
Art historian and critic
General commissioner of the
International Year of Gaudí

Das Phänomen Gaudí

Angesichts der stetig wachsenden Anerkennung des Werkes von Antoni Gaudí i Cornet über 150 Jahre nach seiner Geburt stellt sich die Frage nach dem Grund für dieses in der Architektur ungewöhnliche Phänomen. Gaudís Erfolg beruht nicht auf der Anzahl der von ihm geschaffenen Werke: Er leitete ja nur ungefähr zwanzig bedeutende Projekte. Ebenso wenig kann dieser Erfolg auf eine weite geografische Verbreitung der Gebäude zurückgeführt werden, denn diese befinden sich zum größten Teil im Stadtgebiet von Barcelona. Der Grund besteht auch nicht darin, dass der Autor sein Werk und seine Person ins Rampenlicht gestellt hätte – er lebte stets weit entfernt von allem, was seine Arbeit hätte stören können –, und ebenso wenig darin, dass seine Vorschläge von seinen Zeitgenossen mit Enthusiasmus aufgenommen wurden. Diese standen seinem Schaffen im Allgemeinen eher ablehnend gegenüber. Es ist also nicht einfach, eine vernünftige Antwort zu finden, die sowohl Gaudís gegenwärtigen Bekanntheitsgrad rechtfertigen würde als auch die Tatsache, dass er schon vor seinem Tod im Jahre 1926 in Vergessenheit geraten war.

Vermutlich besteht sein Geheimnis darin, dass er sich architektonischem Schaffen ohne künstlerische oder technische Vorurteile auf andere Weise zu nähern wusste. Seine Kenntnis des Handwerks und der Konstruktionsvorgänge hätten es ihm gestattet, sich in seiner

Epoche hervorzutun, indem er die eklektizistischen Stilmittel in Übereinstimmung mit dem Kanon des 19. Jahrhunderts und den barocken und neo-romantischen Vorlieben des Modernismus anwandte. Er hätte eine berühmte Persönlichkeit sein können wie zum Beispiel Domènech i Montaner oder Puig i Cadafalch, die sich in seiner unmittelbaren Umgebung befanden, oder wie Victor Horta, Hector Guimard, Charles Rennie Mackintosh, Otto Wagner, Josef Hoffmann oder Joseph Maria Olbrich auf europäischem Niveau. Sie alle waren große Architekten mit einer eigenen Formensprache und nehmen daher eine bedeutende Stellung in der Geschichte der Kunst und der Architektur ein. Aber Gaudí wollte mehr: Seine ausgeprägte Individualität ermöglichte es ihm, mit der Tradition zu brechen; gleichzeitig blieb er doch den historischen Stilrichtungen treu, um das anspruchsvolle Bürgertum der Jahrhundertwende zufriedenzustellen.

Er wollte das Wesen der Architektur seiner Zeit infrage stellen und Materialien, Verfahren, Techniken, Berechnungssysteme und geometrische Grundlagen, aber auch ästhetische Ansätze neu überdenken. Dabei ging es ihm nicht darum, alles Vorherige zu verdrängen. Im Gegenteil, da er die architektonischen Mittel sowohl in stilistischer als auch in technischer Hinsicht beherrschte, konnte er sich auf ein persönliches Abenteuer einlassen, auf eine spielerische Intuition, die seinen Arbeiten Unabhängigkeit und Originalität verlieh. Niemand kann behaupten, dass Gaudí ein Erleuchteter gewesen sei, auch wenn einige dies ernsthaft taten und sich auf eine hypothetische Esoterik der von ihm verwendeten Symbolik beriefen. Aber Antoni Gaudí war einer der herausragenden Köpfe im Übergang vom 19. zum 20. Jahrhundert, denn er war sich der Notwendigkeit bewusst, mit historisierendem Romantizismus

abzuschließen, die sich im Europa jener Zeit ausbreiteten. Die Welt veränderte sich, und andere Lebenskonzepte drängten in den Vordergrund, die auch in der Architektur ausgedrückt werden mussten.

Gaudí erlangte 1878 an der anspruchsvollen Escuela Técnica Superior de Arquitectura den Architektentitel. Diese Ausbildung sowie Beherrschung der Fachsprache und Kenntnis der Werkstoffe in den verschiedenen Handwerksberufen, die er bei seinem Vater in Reus und in den besten Werkstätten Barcelonas kennengelernt hatte, befähigten ihn, erste Annäherungsversuche an neo-gotische, arabisierende und ähnliche Formen zu unternehmen, die ihren Höhepunkt in der Casa Vicens in Barcelona erreichten. Dort entwickelte er konstruktive Lösungen, von denen wir heute mit Fug und Recht behaupten können, dass sie der Keim einer unverwechselbaren Aus...

dracksweise sind, die auf geschwungenen Oberflächen, parabolischen, hyperbolischen Formen, spiralförmigen Rhythmen sowie leuchtender Farbigkeit fußt. Weit entfernt von jeglichem Stil der Vergangenheit, gehorcht sie einer Architektur ohne -ismen und kann, wie Gaudís Schüler Martinell sagte, nur als Gaudísmus bezeichnet werden.

In reiferem Alter tendierte Gaudí immer mehr zur empirischen Philosophie, die Realität nur noch als Resultat von Erfahrung zulässt und die ihre Blütezeit während des 18. Jahrhunderts hatte. Seine Experimentierfreude rührt wahrscheinlich auch von dem „gesunden Menschenverstand" her, der die Bauern des Camp de Tarragona auszeichnet: praktisch veranlagte Menschen, die sich ihrer Arbeit widmen und sparsam mit ihren Mitteln und ihrer Energie umgehen. Gaudí stellte das Vorgehen des Architekten allgemein auf den Prüf...

stand. Er machte seine Werkstätten zu Laboratorien, arbeitete mit experimentellen Modellen, suchte nach widerstandsfähigen Stoffen wie Granit, Basalt und Porphyr, schlug geschwungene Wände und Decken vor, entschied sich für schräge Säulen, interessierte sich für den Verlauf des Lichtes und die Belüftung der Gebäude, berechnete die Struktur seiner Bauten mittels Kettenbögen, verwendete Spiegel, Fotografie und die nicht euklidische Geometrie zum Entwerfen von Rauminhalten … Dieser Wagemut, der viele überrascht und den nicht alle verstehen, ließ so beeindruckende Bauwerke wie die Kirche der Colònia Güell, die Pedrera, den Park Güell oder die Sagrada Família entstehen. All diese Werke waren der leichtfertigen Kritik der Öffentlichkeit und der Medien ausgesetzt, beeindruckten jedoch stets durch ihre ungewöhnliche Kraft. Francesc Pujols, ein bekannter Philosoph jener Zeit und Freund

Gaudís, behauptet, dass „es bei allen Werken Gaudís so sei, dass sie, auch wenn sie niemandem gefielen, so beschaffen waren, dass gleichzeitig keiner wagte, ihm dies offen ins Gesicht zu sagen, da er einen Stil hatte, der sich durchsetzte, ohne zu gefallen“. Diese Behauptung muss heute revidiert werden, da Gaudís Projekte nicht nur immer noch Verblüffung hervorrufen, sondern darüber hinaus auf breiter Ebene immer mehr zu Kultobjekten erklärt wurden.

Daran ist deutlich zu erkennen, dass Gaudí weiterhin lebendig ist. Einige seiner Gebäude wurden von der UNESCO zu kunsthistorischen Denkmälern und Weltkulturerbestätten erklärt. Die meisten von ihnen wurden restauriert und wiederhergestellt und gingen von privater in öffentliche Nutzung über. Bereits zu seiner Zeit prophezeite Gaudí, dass in der Casa Milà, besser bekannt als Pedrera, letztendlich ein großes Hotel oder ein Kongresspalast untergebracht wurde. Dies bewahrheitete sich im Jahr 1996, als ein Finanzinstitut das Gebäude in ein Kulturzentrum umwandelte. Es ist nicht das einzige Gebäude, das einem anderen Zweck zugeführt wurde: Die Remisen-Pavillons der Finca Güell sind heute Sitz des Königlichen Gaudí-Lehrstuhls der Universitat Politècnica de Catalunya; der Palau Güell, Wohnsitz seiner Mäzene, der Park Güell, die Sagrada Família und die Kirche der Colònia Güell sind für die Öffentlichkeit zugänglich. Casa Calvet beherbergt im Untergeschoss ein Restaurant, in dem das Originalmobiliar erhalten ist, Casa Batlló ist ein Versammlungszentrum und teilweise für Besucher geöffnet. Wie bereits erwähnt, ist die Pedrera ein Kulturzentrum mit Ausstellungsraum, Auditorium, einer Wohnung im Stil der damaligen Zeit und dem Dokumentationszentrum des Espai Gaudí auf der Dachterrasse. Der Bischofspalast von Astorga beherbergt ein Museum, die Casa de los Botines in León den Sitz eines Finanzinstituts und dessen Dauerausstellungsräume und El Capricho in Comillas ein Restaurant.

Hat auch jedes einzelne Werk eine Metamorphose durchgemacht, so ist Gaudís Arbeit weiterhin präsent. Um den Architekten und Künstler zu würdigen, muss man seine Gebäude besuchen und sein Werk kennenlernen. Nur so können wir den Zusammenhang verstehen, der zwischen seinen Konstruktionssystemen, seinen bewohnbaren Räumen, seinen Fassaden und Dächern besteht. Gaudí ist unteilbares Ganzes: Logik der Form und Erhöhung der Kunst.

Daniel Giralt-Miracle
Kritiker und Kunsthistoriker,
Generalkommissar des Internationalen
Gaudí-Jahres

Nature, technique, and artistry

Gaudí grew up in Camp de Tarragona, an area planted with vineyards and olive trees, dotted with small villages and rocky massifs. Gaudí's capacity to observe the landscape during his childhood gave him a special vision of the world. His surroundings brought together all of the laws of construction and structure that the architect needed to create his buildings.

Gaudí's brilliant mind found information and inspiration in nature. For example, the arches in the attics of his buildings are similar to the skeletons of vertebrates, and the columns of the Sagrada Família branch out like trees. All of Gaudí's buildings reinterpret the norms that regulate the creation of the universe.

Modernist architects often reproduced floral motifs, though Gaudí's use of nature in his work reflected a global attitude that exceeded the abstractions used in modernist decorations.

Gaudí relied on the simplicity and immediacy of nature to solve architectural problems. He distrusted complex mathematical calculations and chose empirical verifications instead. This method led him to conduct numerous experiments to calculate the load of a structure or the final form of a decoration. The model was the ideal instrument.

Gaudí's passion for organic structures explains the absence of reinforced concrete and steel in his

buildings. These materials are only valuable when using numerical calculations. Gaudí's brilliant construction ideas could only be realized with materials like wood, stone, or wrought iron. Therefore, he also surrounded himself with specialized artists and artisans.

With ceramics, Gaudí relied on the invaluable advice of Manuel Vicens i Montaner, who commissioned the architect to build his residence.

Filigrees of wrought iron appear in all of Gaudí's works. The door of the Güell estate, manufactured by the Vallet i Piqué workshop, is the most emblematic example.

Gaudí's use of wood also led him to rely on artisans of the era who could transform his imaginative designs into reality. Of particular interest are the doors and screens of the Casa Batlló created by Casas y Bardés, and the level ceilings of the Casa Vicens, full of vegetable motifs.

The architect and his qualified collaborators also created magnificent works out of other materials such as plaster, stone, brick, and glass. The innovative applications, the undulating forms, and the new functions for which he used the materials simply would not have been possible without the participation of these skilled artisans. Through all his life, his relationship with renowned sculptors, such as Carles Mani, Josep Llimona, and Llorenç Matamala, also led to spectacular combinations that fuse technique and art.

Natur, Technik und Handwerk

Gaudí wuchs im Camp de Tarragona auf, einer steinigen Landschaft voller Weingärten, Oliven- und Affenbrotbäumen mit verstreuten Dörfern und Felsmassiven. In seiner Kindheit verlor er sich häufig in dieser Umgebung, was ihn später zu einer eigentümlichen Weltsicht führte: Die Tier- und Pflanzenwelt enthielten für ihn alle baulichen und strukturellen Gesetze, die ein Architekt zur Planung benötigte.

Die Inspiration, die Gaudí als Gegengewicht zu seiner überschäumenden Fantasie brauchte, fand er in der Natur. Ein gutes Beispiel sind Ähnlichkeiten zwischen der Anordnung der Bögen in den Dachgeschossen und den Knochengerüsten der Wirbeltiere, oder aber die Form der Säulen der Sagrada Família, die sich wie Äste eines Baumes verzweigen. Sämtliche Gebäude Gaudís interpretieren die Gesetzmäßigkeiten der Erschaffung des Universums neu, indem sie den Architekten mit dem Schöpfer vergleichen.

Die Darstellung floraler Motive war ein von Architekten eingesetztes Mittel, wobei hervorzuheben ist, dass die Natur im Werk Gaudís eine umfassendere Rolle spielt, die über Abstraktionen in den modernistischen Ornamenten weit hinausgeht.

Gaudí verließ sich auf Einfachheit und Unmittelbarkeit der Naturbetrachtung beim Lösen architektonischer Probleme.

Komplexe mathematische Berechnungen erweckten sein Misstrauen. Er führte Experimente zur Bestimmung der Traglasten oder der Form eines Ornaments durch und setzte Modelle in naturgetreuem Maßstab für verschiedene Gestaltungsprozesse ein.

Gaudís Vorliebe für organische Strukturen erklärt das Fehlen von Stahl und Beton – Werkstoffe, die kostspielig waren und Berechnungen notwendig machten. Seine Ideen als Baumeister ließen sich nur mit Holz, Naturstein oder Gusseisen umsetzen. Darum umgab er sich mit Künstlern und Handwerkern, die auf diese Materialien spezialisiert waren.

Beim Einsatz von Keramik konnte er auf Ratschläge des barcelonischen Keramikers Manuel Vicens i Montaner zurückgreifen.

Filigrane Arbeiten aus Schmiedeeisen finden sich an sämtlichen Werken Gaudís, beispielsweise die in der Werkstatt von Vallet i Piqué hergestellte Tür der Finca Güell.

Der Einsatz von Holz war ein weiterer Berührungspunkt mit den Handwerkern seiner Zeit. Sie verwirklichten seine fantasiereichsten Entwürfe. Hier sind besonders Türen und Trennwände der Casa Batlló hervorzuheben, die bei Casas y Bardés in Auftrag gegeben wurden, sowie Pflanzenmotive an den Decken der Casa Vicens.

Nicht zu vergessen sind auch die Arbeiten aus Gips, Stein, Ziegelstein und Glas, die der engagierten Mitarbeit qualifizierter Handwerker zu verdanken sind. Die neuartigen Anwendungen, die geschwungenen Formen und die außergewöhnlichen Funktionen wären ohne deren fruchtbare Hilfe unmöglich gewesen. Er hat berühmte Bildhauer wie Carles Mani, Josep Llimona und Llorenç Matamala zur Mitarbeit herangezogen.

The life of Gaudí

Das Leben Gaudís

The life of Gaudí

On the afternoon of June 7, 1926, a distracted old man, immersed in his thoughts, was wandering around Barcelona. At the corner of Gran Via and Carrer Bailèn, he was struck by a tram.

The victim carried no documentation in his coat, making it impossible to identify him. Though he was still breathing, he was badly hurt and covered with blood. He lay on the ground next to the tracks. Mistaken for a beggar, the dying old man was transported by ambulance to Hospital de la Santa Creu, where all the city's vagabonds and poor people were taken. Three days after being admitted to the hospital, the old man died from the fatal blow, in a small and empty room. Antoni Gaudí had passed away.

The day of the funeral, Saturday, June 12, was a sad day for the numerous residents of Barcelona that followed the silent procession through the city from Hospital de la Santa Creu to the Sagrada Família, a church also known as the "cathedral of the poor", where he was buried in the crypt.

Antoni Gaudí was born 74 years earlier in the city of Reus (in the province of Tarragona). Reus was then the second most important city in Catalonia in terms of population, and also was one of the most active commercial and industrial centers in southern Europe.

On June 25, 1852, a humble family of tinkers, the Gaudí Cornets, had their fifth and last child: Antoni Plàcid Guillem Gaudí i Cornet. Gaudí's older siblings were Rosa (1844–1879), Maria (1845–1850), Francesc (1848–1850), and Francesc (1851–1876). Antoni's brothers and sisters died young and he was the only child to outlive his parents. Rosa was the only one to marry and produce descendants, a girl named Rosa Egea Gaudí.

From early on, Antoni exhibited a sickliness that deeply affected his infancy and conditioned his habits throughout his life. Starting at the age of five, the youngest member of the Gaudí Cornet family suffered severe pains that obliged him to stay at home for long periods of time. Doctors diagnosed his condition as arthritis, which often impeded his ability to walk. Instead of running and playing like other children, Gaudí learned to understand and see the world with different eyes. He was deeply attracted to nature and was capable of spending hours contemplating stones, plants, flowers, insects…

At the age of 11, Gaudí began his studies at the Escuelas Pías in

Reus, a free religious school located in the old convent of Sant Francesc designated for the education of the lower classes. This is when he probably began to develop his fervent faith and devotion.

During his high-school years, Gaudí's performance was not remarkable; in fact, his student record, which still exists today, shows that the young man failed one or two classes and earned mediocre grades. Withdrawn, solitary, serious and difficult, Gaudí's restless mind found it hard to adjust to the authoritarian system, school discipline, and established norms. During this time, he became strongly

attracted to drawing and architecture and had tremendous ability for manual work.

With his mind set on architecture, Gaudí finished school and moved to Barcelona. At the age of 21, he was admitted to the Escola Tècnica Superior d'Arquitectura and began his career. In 1876, shortly after Antoni had begun his architecture studies, his brother Francesc died, followed by his mother a few months later. During the rest of his studies, Gaudí would share living quarters with his father and his niece Rosa Egea, the only family that he had left and would ever have.

As in high school, Gaudí was not a top student and received his best grades for drawings and projects.

In 1878, with his diploma in his hand, Gaudí was beginning to be in demand, and he completed an array of assignments such as a kiosk, a wall, a wrought iron gate and a roof with columns for the theater of Sant Gervasi, and a glass showcase exhibited at the Spanish Pavilion of the Universal Exhibition in Paris that same year.

The same year Gaudí graduated from university, Barcelona's City Hall selected him to design street lampposts. Gaudí created the street lamps with six arms that are currently to be found in Barcelona's Plaça Reial, and others with three arms located in Pla de Palau.

Gaudí's first big assignment came from Salvador Pagès, a worker born in Reus who amassed a fortune in the USA. Pagès, director of the workers' cooperative of Mataró, wanted to build a residential development for the workers. He was only able to build a small part of the project, which deeply disappointed him.

A veteran architect, Martorell was aware of his assistant and protégé's potential and talent; he introduced the architect to the man who would become his patron and one of his best friends and clients: Eusebi Güell i Bacigalupi.

Eusebi Güell, son of Joan Güell Ferrer, one of the driving forces behind Catalan industry and a leader of Catalan economic thought, inherited business sense from his father and a passion for arts and culture from his mother. In 1878 he attended the Universal Exhibition in Paris, where a splendid display caught his attention. When he returned to Barcelona, he discovered the designer of the work. The friendship between Güell and Gaudí lasted until the businessman's death in 1917. Both felt deeply Catalan and their nationalism inspired them to promote the Catalan culture and language, even when it was prohibited. These nationalist feelings are represented in many of Gaudí's designs, including sculptures and coats of arms which feature the four bars of the "senyera" (the Catalan flag) or other symbolic elements.

The first assignment that Gaudí accepted from Güell was a hunting pavilion that Güell wanted to build on a property near Barcelona. Projects of greater magnitude followed, including an urban palace situated near La Rambla in Barcelona, a summer estate, and a colony, among others. However, these were not Gaudí's only assignments, given that the architect alternated buildings for his mentor with other commissions, such as a house for Manuel Vicens, a summer residence in Comillas for Máximo Díaz de Quijano, and the Theresian school.

Once Gaudí had become a close friend of Güell, he increased his assignments, fees and circle of acquaintances. He entered a prolific period of creative production that led to a personalized language and style.

In 1883, his friend Joan Martorell was trying to find an architect to take over the construction of the Temple of the Sagrada Família. Construction had begun in 1882. Josep Bocabella was in charge of raising the money for the construction of the expiatory church, which could only be financed by donations. The architect in charge of the project was Francisco de Paula del Villar, Gaudí's former professor. As soon as the construction of the crypt began, Villar and Bocabella had disagreements and Villar resigned. Joan Martorell, Bocabella's assessor, proposed Gaudí for the job. Bocabella did not object to the solution because he trusted the veteran architect and the plans for the project which was interrupted on the project were already finished. Gaudí combined other assignments with the works of the Sagrada Família until 1914, when he dedicated himself exclusively to it.

From then on, Gaudí did not accept any other commissions and isolated himself from everything that might distract him from his obsession. He devoted his life to the construction of what he once said would be the "first cathedral of a new series." He even moved to live right next to the cathedral to save time and work more.

The aging architect had dedicated his life to God and to a June 7, 1926, due to an unfortunate accident. Gaudí paid so little attention to his appearance that he looked like a vagabond. After being hit by a tram, he lay on the ground, badly wounded.

No one paid attention to the supposed beggar except one man, the textile merchant Ángel Tomás Mohino, whose identity was recently discovered. He and another passer-by helped the victim, trying to hail taxis to take him to a hospital but had no luck. In the hospital for the poor, the genius died in a desolate room three days after the fatal accident.

Das Leben Gaudís

Am Mittag des 7. Juni 1926 spazierte ein älterer Mann zerstreut und in Gedanken versunken durch das Zentrum von Barcelona. An der Straßenecke Gran Via und Carrer Bailèn wurde er von einer Straßenbahn angefahren.

Da der Verunglückte keine Ausweispapiere in seiner Jacke trug, konnten die Personalien nicht festgestellt werden. Der sterbende Mann wurde für einen Bettler gehalten und im Krankenwagen in das Krankenhaus Hospital de la Santa Creu gebracht. Drei Tage nach seiner Einlieferung starb er an den Folgen des Unfalls, ohne Nachkommen zu hinterlassen.

Der Tag des Begräbnisses – Samstag, 12. Juni 1926 – war ein trauriger Tag für zahlreiche Bürger Barcelonas, die dem Trauerzug auf seinem Weg durch die Straßen vom Krankenhaus Hospital de la Santa Creu bis zur Sagrada Família folgten. Dort sollte Gaudí in der Krypta beerdigt werden. Auf der Strecke herrschte vollkommene Stille.

Antoni Gaudí kam 74 Jahre zuvor in der Provinz Tarragona in Reus zur Welt. Am 25. Juni 1852 wurde im bescheidenen Heim einer Familie von Kupferschmieden, dem der Eheleute Gaudí Cornet, das fünfte und letzte Kind geboren: Antoni

Barcelona's Plaça de Catalunya at the beginning of the 20th Century. Nearly is the church of Sant Felip Neri, which the architect usually attended.

Die Plaça de Catalunya in Barcelona Anfang des 20. Jahrhunderts. Ganz in der Nähe befindet sich die Kirche Sant Felip Neri, die der Architekt häufig besuchte.

Plàcid Guillem Gaudí i Corniet. Zuvor waren Rosa (1844–1879), Maria (1845–1850), Francesc (1848–1850) und Francesc (1851–1876) auf die Welt gekommen. Antoni war der Einzige, der seine Eltern überlebte. Die Einzige, die Nachkommen hatte, war Rosa, die heiratete und eine Tochter bekam.

Obwohl Antoni ein hohes Alter erreichte, war er schon von klein auf kränklich, was seine Kindheit zutiefst prägte. Er musste zum Beispiel eine strenge vegetarische Diät einhalten und möglichst oft spazieren gehen.

Ab dem fünften Lebensjahr litt er unter starken Schmerzen, die ihn immer wieder über lange Zeiträume

zwangen, zu Hause zu bleiben. Die Gelenk-Arthritis, welche die Ärzte bei ihm feststellten, machte ihm das Gehen oft unmöglich. Anstatt wie die meisten Kinder zu laufen, zu springen oder zu spielen, lernte er früh, seine Umgebung und die Welt mit anderen Augen zu betrachten. Die Natur zog ihn stark an, und er beobachtete stundenlang Steine, Pflanzen, Blumen, Insekten und andere Tiere.

Mit elf Jahren begann Gaudí seine Ausbildung an der Schule Escuelas Pías in Reus, einer Schule im alten Konvent des Heiligen Franziskus, die sich der Erziehung widmete. Gaudí kam hier mit der römisch-katholischen Religion in sich beim Lernen nicht hervor. Zurückgezogen, einsam, Scherzen abgeneigt und von schwierigem Charakter, fiel es seinem unruhigen Geist von Jugend an schwer, sich an das autoritäre System, an die schulische Disziplin und die herrschenden Normen anzupassen. In jener Zeit fühlte er sich zum Zeichnen und zur Architektur hingezogen und besaß großes Geschick für Handarbeiten.

an teilte er die Wohnsitze, die er während seiner Ausbildung hatte, mit seinem Vater und seiner Nichte Rosa Egea. Sie bildeten seine Familie, da er nie heiratete.

Genauso wie in seiner Zeit als Abiturient war Gaudí kein herausragender Student an der Universität. 1878, mit dem Titel in der Tasche, wurde Gaudí aber bald ein gefragter Architekt; unter seinen Entwürfen befanden sich ein Kiosk, eine Mauer, ein Zaun, das Säulendach für ein Theater in Sant Gervasi und ein Glasschaufenster, das auf der Weltausstellung in Paris im spanischen Pavillon ausgestellt wurde.

Im Jahr seines Studienabschlusses wurde er von der Stadtverwaltung von Barcelona dazu ersucht, Gaslaternen für die Straßenbeleuchtung zu entwerfen. Ergebnisse von Gaudís Schaffen waren die sechsarmigen Laternen, die heute noch auf der Plaça Reial in Barcelona stehen, sowie die dreiarmigen auf dem Pla de Palau.

Seinen ersten großen Auftrag erhielt Gaudí aus der Hand von Salvador Pagès, einem in Reus

geborenen Arbeiter, der es in den USA zu großem Vermögen gebracht hatte. Pagès, der Leiter der Arbeitergenossenschaft von Mataró, wollte dort eine Anlage mit Einzelwohnhäusern für Arbeiter erschaffen. Es wurde letztendlich jedoch nur ein kleiner Teil der in Auftrag gegebenen Gebäude errichtet, was Gaudí tief enttäuschte.

Gaudís Mentor, der Architekt Joan Martorell, erkannte jedoch die enormen Fähigkeiten seines Schützlings und stellte ihn dem Mann vor, der sein Mäzen und einer seiner besten Freunde und Kunden werden sollte: Eusebi Güell i Bacigalupi.

Der Sohn Joan Güell Ferrers, einer der treibenden Kräfte und Vordenker der katalanischen Industrie, der den ausgeprägten Geschäftssinn seines Vaters, von seiner Mutter hingegen die große Leidenschaft für Kunst und Kultur geerbt hatte, verstand etwas von Musik, Bildhauerei und Malerei. 1878 hatte er die Weltausstellung in Paris besucht, wo eine Glasvitrine seine Aufmerksamkeit weckte. Zurück in Barcelona fand er heraus, dass Gaudí sie entworfen hatte.

Die zwischen Güell und Gaudí entstehende Freundschaft hielt bis zum Tod des Unternehmers 1918. Beide besaßen eine tiefes Nationalgefühl als Katalanen, das sie dazu brachte, die katalanische Sprache und Kultur stets zu fördern, auch, als dies offiziell verboten war. Dies kommt in vielen Werken zum Ausdruck: in Skulpturen, im Wappen mit den vier Streifen, der „senyera" genannten katalanischen Flagge und anderen symbolischen Elementen.

Der erste Auftrag von Gaudís späterem Förderer war ein Jagdpavillon auf einem Grundstück, das Güell in der Nähe von Barcelona besaß. Daraus ergaben sich weitere Aufträge von größerer Tragweite, zum Beispiel der Stadtpalast in der Nähe der Rambla von Barcelona, eine Sommerresidenz und eine Siedlung.

Gaudí unterbrach die Arbeiten für seinen Mentor oft für andere Aufträge, wie das Haus für den Ziegelsteinfabrikanten Manuel Vicens, die Sommerresidenz für Máximo Díaz de Quijano in Comillas oder das Colegio de las Teresianas.

Seit Gaudís Freundschaft mit Güell steigerten sich mit seinen Aufträgen auch seine Honorare und sein Bekanntheitsgrad. Er durchlebte eine sehr fruchtbare Schaffensperiode, die ihn mit wachsender Erfahrung zu der für ihn charakteristischen Sprache finden ließ.

1883 suchte Joan Martorell einen Architekten für die Arbeiten an der Sagrada Família. Josep Bocabella

war beauftragt, das für den Bau notwendige Geld aufzubringen.

Der mit dem Projekt betraute Architekt war der ehemalige Professor Francisco de Paula del Villar. Zu Beginn der Arbeiten an der Krypta kam es zu Auseinandersetzungen zwischen Villar und Bocabella, die zum Rücktritt Villars führten. Joan Martorell, zu jener Zeit Assistent Bocabellas, schlug Gaudí für die Leitung der Bauarbeiten vor. Gegen diese Lösung hatte Bocabella aus zwei Gründen nichts einzuwenden: Auf der einen Seite hatte er vollstes Vertrauen in den Architekten, auf der anderen handelte es sich eigentlich um eine Routinearbeit, da sämtliche Zeichnungen für das Projekt bereits fertig gestellt waren.

Von jetzt an stimmte Gaudí seine neuen Aufträge mit den Arbeiten an der Sagrada Família ab, bis er 1914 den Entschluss fasste, sich ausschließlich dieser Aufgabe zu widmen, von der er sagte, dass es „die erste Kathedrale einer neuen Serie" sei. Der geniale Künstler verlegte sogar seinen Wohnsitz in die unmittelbare Nähe der Baustelle, damit er sich Wege sparen und die Zeit besser nutzen konnte. Er verbrachte den Rest seines Lebens vollständig versunken in die Arbeiten an der Kirche.

Am 7. Juni 1926 wurden diese aufgrund eines tragischen Unfalls unterbrochen. Gaudí, der sein Äußeres so vernachlässigt hatte, dass er wie ein Landstreicher aussah, wurde von einer Straßenbahn erfasst und blieb schwer verletzt auf der Straße liegen.

Niemand schenkte dem mutmaßlichen Bettler Beachtung. Nur ein Mann, der Textilhändler Ángel Tomás Mohino, leistete dem Verletzten zusammen mit einem weiteren Passanten Hilfe. Sie bemühten sich, ein Taxi anzuhalten, um den Verunglückten ins Krankenhaus transportieren zu können, doch ohne Erfolg. Das Genie starb drei Tage später in einem Armenkrankenhaus.

The way he was
Wie war er?

Gaudí's humble origins often influenced his life and behavior. Despite feeling profoundly united to his people, during his youth Gaudí was attracted to high-society life, although at the end of his days, he lived without any luxuries.

Gaudí had a strong complexion, pronounced cheekbones, aprominent forehead, a distinctive nose and a rural sturdiness disguised by his blond hair and deep-blue eyes.

Though Gaudí had an imposing figure, he was shy, had a difficult character and a strong temperament. He was conscious of his bad temper, and often felt no need to conceal it.

Er war ein Mann von kräftiger Statur, mit markanten Wangenknochen, vorspringender Stirn und ausgeprägter Nase. Dieses robuste Äußere trat zurück hinter seinem blonden Haar, das in seiner Jugend ins Rötliche ging und im Laufe der Jahre weiß wurde. Er hatte einen rosigen Teint und tiefblaue Augen, deren Blick durchdringend und war und einen in den Bann zog. Sein imposantes nordisches Aussehen unterschied ihn schon von klein auf von seinen Schulkameraden und wurde von ihm selbst abgelehnt. Er rebellierte dagegen und betonte stets, dass er vom Mittelmeer stamme und Katalane sei.

Gaudí, a freemason?
Gaudí, ein Freimaurer?

Gaudí has been labeled an alchemist, a Templar, a drug addict... but there is no evidence to prove any of this. One of the most widespread theories is his association with Freemasonry. Many have examined his work in the search for details to prove it, such as his obsession for certain elements and the fact that he surrounded himself with people who belonged to the masonry lodge, like Eduard and Josep Fontserè, with whom he worked. It is difficult to believe that an architect with a Catholic education, who projected so many religious buildings and objects, would be capable of living this double life.

Viele Dinge sind über den katalanischen Architekten geschrieben und gesagt worden, die meisten davon sind reine Vermutungen. Einer der am weitesten verbreiteten Theorien zufolge war er Anhänger der Freimaurerei. Viele haben in seinem Werk nach Hinweisen dafür gesucht. Die Besessenheit Gaudís von bestimmten Elementen oder die Tatsache, dass er sich mit Personen umgab, die wirklich der Freimaurerloge angehörten, könnten darauf hin deuten. Es ist jedoch schwer vorzustellbar, dass ein Architekt, der religiöse Gebäude und Gegenstände entwarf, zu einem solchen Doppelleben fähig gewesen sein soll.

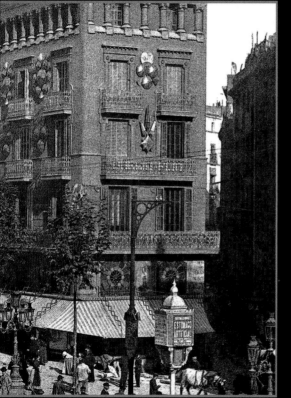

Near this location, la Rambla dels Caputxins, Gaudí constructed an urban palace for his patron, the industrialist Eusebi Güell.

In der Nähe dieses Abschnitts der Rambla dels Caputxins, errichtete Antoni Gaudí einen Stadtpalast für seinen Mäzen, den Industriellen Eusebi Güell.

Beatification?
Seligsprechung?

Undeniably, Gaudí was a devoutly religious man. Many have seen in him the figure of an exemplary Christian, almost a saint. Some time ago, the process for his beatification was set in motion, with a view to his eventual canonization. The proposal was well received by the Vatican, which authorized a beatification process that entails a long and difficult road of analyzing the pros and cons before reaching a final conclusion. Saint or not, it is certain that Gaudí's tomb has become a destination for devotees who have converted it into a place of pilgrimage.

Es ist unstrittig, dass Gaudí ein tief gläubiger Mensch mit einem ausgeprägten Sinn für Religiosität war. Viele sehen in ihm einen beispielhaften Christen, fast schon einen Heiligen. Daher gibt es seit einiger Zeit Bemühungen, seine Selig- und anschließende Heiligsprechung zu veranlassen. Der Heilige Stuhl hat den Vorschlag wohlwollend angenommen und das Verfahren zur Seligsprechung genehmigt. Nun beginnt der langwierige Prozess. Ob Heiliger oder nicht – das Grab Gaudís wird von immer mehr Verehrern besucht, die es schon jetzt zu einem Pilgerort gemacht haben.

Bandi

Constructed works

Realisierte Projekte

Casa Vicens

1883-1888

In 1883, the young Gaudí accepted one of his first commissions as an architect. Situated at number 24–26 on Carrer Carolines, in the neighborhood of Gràcia, Casa Vicens is a magnificent building that mixes Spanish architectural forms (inspired by medieval architecture) with Arabic elements. The architectural style is more similar to Moorish art than to the French School which tended to set the trends of the era.

The project, commissioned by Manuel Vicens, entailed the construction of a summer residence with a garden. The architect envisioned Casa Vicens as a subtle combination of geometric volumes. Resolved with skill and mastery, the building features horizontal bands on the lower part, and vertical lines, accentuated by varnished ceramics, as ornamentation on the upper part.

The building, with a square floor plan and two stories, is smaller than it seems. For the exterior walls, Gaudí opted to use simple materials: ochre-colored natural stone as a base element combined with bricks. The result of this combination is that the brick stands out as a decorative element, as do the multicolored tiles that extend along the wall in a pattern similar to that of a chessboard. The colored ceramics and the small towers give the composition an Arabic feel, which contrasts pleasantly with the window gratings, the small balconies and the modernist forms of the wrought-iron garden gates.

In 1925, the architect J.B. Serra de Martínez enlarged the house, respecting the criteria, forms, and colors used by Gaudí.

Im Jahr 1883 erhielt Gaudí seinen ersten Auftrag als Architekt. Die Casa Vicens befindet sich im Stadtviertel Gràcia und ist ein Bauwerk, dessen Formen sich – von der mittelalterlichen Baukunst Spaniens inspiriert – mit Elementen arabischen Charakters mischen, die eher der Mudéjar-Kunst zuzuordnen sind als zeitgenössischen Bauten, die maßgeblich von der französischen Schule beeinflusst waren.

Das von dem Keramik- und Ziegelsteinfabrikanten Manuel Vicens in Auftrag gegebene Projekt bestand darin, eine Sommerresidenz mit Garten zu bauen. Der Architekt plante mit meisterlichem Können die subtile Kombination von geometrischen Bestandteilen, um waagerechte Streifen im unteren Teil des Gebäudes mit senkrechten Linien im oberen Teil in Einklang zu bringen.

Das quadratische Haus aus zwei Stockwerken ist kleiner, als es scheint. Für die Außenmauern wählte er Materialien wie ockerfarbenen Naturstein in Verbindung mit Ziegelstein. Dadurch sticht der Ziegelstein als ornamentales Element hervor, ebenso wie bunte Kacheln, deren Anordnung einem Schachbrett gleicht. Keramik und Türmchen verleihen der Komposition ein arabisches Flair, das mit den modernistischen Formen des schmiedeeisernen Zaunes, den Balkonen oder den Gittern vor den Fenstern kontrastiert. Die Gartenlaube, der monumentale Springbrunnen mit einem Parabolbogen aus unverputztem Ziegelstein und ein Teil des Gartens fielen dem Straßenausbau zum Opfer.

1925 erweiterte der Architekt J. B. Serra de Martínez das Haus und zitierte dabei die von Gaudí verwendeten Kriterien, Formen und Farben.

With the Casa Vicens, Gaudí's first residential project in Barcelona, the architect proposed an interesting fusion between architecture and the plastic arts. He would repeat this combination throughout his career.

Mit der Casa Vicens, seinem erstem Hausprojekt in Barcelona, zeigt Gaudí erstmals eine interessante Verschmelzung von Architektur und plastischer Kunst, die sich durch seine gesamte produktive und kreative Karriere zieht.

Gaudí emulated the Moorish style and resolved one of his first works with great skill. Outstanding features include the striking and generous ceramic ornamentation of the façade and the stunning wrought-iron work of the front gate, balconies, banisters, and window gratings.

Durch Nachempfinden des maurischen Stils löste Antoni Gaudí einen seiner ersten Aufträge auf meisterhafte Art und Weise. Den aufsehenerregenden, großzügigen Keramikschmuck der Fassade ergänzen die sorgfältigen Schmiedeeisenarbeiten an dem großen Gitter der Eingangstür, den Balkonen, den Geländern und Fenstergittern.

The dynamic composition features attractive geometric combinations determined with skill, and alternating, repeating chromatic designs.

Die dynamischen Kompositionen entstehen aus gekonnten Kombinationen geometrischer Formen sowie einander abwechselnden farbigen Designs.

Lavishly decorated ceilings are one of the architect's trademarks. For this room, situated in a gallery connected to the dining room, Gaudí combined two vaults painted with the trompe l'oeil technique. The drawings represent branches of palm trees, and two adjacent vaults are also decorated copiously with vegetable motifs.

Großzügig dekorierte Decken gehören zu Gaudís Markenzeichen. Für diesen Raum in der Galerie kombinierte Gaudí zwei mit der Trompe-l'œil-Technik bemalte Gewölbe. Die Bilder stellen Palmwedel dar. Zwei angrenzende Gewölbe sind ebenfalls reich mit Pflanzenmotiven verziert.

Diverse forms inspired by vegetable and floral motifs accentuate the decoration of the baroque interiors. For example, in the smoking room, Gaudí covered the walls with papier-mâché, and the vaulted ceiling copies the style of Islamic constructions. Each bay of the vault is covered with plaster and carved to simulate the leaf of a palm tree.

Unterschiedliche, von Blumen- und Pflanzenmotiven inspirierte Formen heben die Dekoration der ausdrucksstarken barocken Innenräume hervor. Im Rauchsalon verkleidete er die Wände mit Pappmaschee, die gewölbte Zwischendecke ahmt den Stil islamischer Bauweise nach.

Villa Quijano
El Capricho

1883-1885

The owner of this property, Máximo Díaz de Quijano, wanted a country house adapted to his needs as a bachelor. This whim caused Villa Quijano to be known as El Capricho (or The Caprice).

The construction, located on the outskirts of Comillas, Santander, sits in an isolated area of the countryside. Villa Quijano shares certain characteristics with other projects of the period such as Casa Vicens in Barcelona. El Capricho demonstrates a definite predominance of curved lines and conjugates typical Spanish medieval architecture with oriental elements.

The Catalan architect paid special attention to the interior spatial organization so that it would adapt to the needs of its owner, and also created an inclined roof that adapts to the climatic conditions of the region, where rain is frequent.

The compact building rises from a solid stone base. The alternating ochre and red bricks are enhanced by rows of green varnished tiles interspersed with ceramic pieces with reliefs of sunflowers. The strength of the composition is broken by the light and svelte tower that presides over it, but seems to have no apparent function. The tower is elevated above a small lookout formed by the four thick columns that support it. The slim tower is crowned by a unique and diminutive roof sustained by light metal supports that seem to defy the laws of gravity and give the building the appearance of typical minarets of Muslim mosques.

Máximo Díaz de Quijano, der Eigentümer dieses Hauses, wünschte sich einen Landsitz, der seinen Bedürfnissen angepasst war. Das Haus wurde unter dem Namen El Capricho bekannt.

Das Bauwerk steht inmitten der Landschaft außerhalb von Comillas (Santander). In seiner Bauart sind Ähnlichkeiten mit einem anderen Werk des Architekten aus derselben Periode festzustellen, der Casa Vicens in Barcelona: Bei El Capricho, im Vergleich zurückhaltender und nüchterner, herrschen geschwungene Linien vor, die gegenüber Geraden immer mehr an Gewicht gewinnen. Auch hier zeigt sich das Bestreben, Formen der mittelalterlichen Bauweise mit Elementen orientalischer Reminiszenz zu vereinen.

Der katalanische Architekt widmete der Aufteilung der Innenräume besondere Aufmerksamkeit, um den Wünschen des Eigentümers zu entsprechen, und baute außen ein Giebeldach, das den klimatischen Bedingungen der Region mit häufigen Niederschlägen angepasst war.

Das kompakte Gebäude ruht auf einem soliden Steinsockel und ist aus rötlichen und ockerfarbenen Ziegelsteinmauern errichtet, die mit Reihen glasierter Kacheln – abwechselnd Sonnenblumenblüten und -blätter – geschmückt sind. Der robuste Komplex wird durch den leichten, schlanken Turm unterbrochen, der, obwohl beherrschend, keine sichtbare Funktion hat. Er wird von einem ungewöhnlichen Dach gekrönt, das auf leichten Metallträgern ruht, die den Gesetzen der Schwerkraft zu trotzen scheinen und dem Ganzen eine eigentümliche Ähnlichkeit mit muslimischen Minaretten verleihen.

A svelte tower rises up from four heavy columns. The tower has no apparent function, yet dominates the composition. A cylindrical trunk covered with ceramics supports a small wrought-iron balustrade crowned by a small shrine.

Aus vier soliden Säulen erwächst der mit Kacheln verkleidete Turm, der keine ersichtliche Funktion hat. Er wird von einer schmiedeeisernen Balustrade abgeschlossen, die von einem Miniaturtempel gekrönt wird.

The solid lines of the projecting corner balconies, made of stone, are softened by the covering, which is made of square steel bars and light rails. When the lines coincide at an angle, they become original wrought-iron benches.

Die markanten Linien der auskragenden Balkone werden durch schmiedeeiserne Gitter gemildert. Ein System von Metallrohren, die als Gegengewicht eingebaut sind, erzeugt beim Öffnen und Schließen der Schiebefenster Töne.

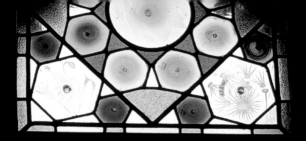

Gaudí paid special attention to the interiors of the residence, especially to their organization and decorative details. The spatial distribution was perfectly adapted to the needs of the owner, a young bachelor. The building was purchased in 1992 by a Japanese group that runs a restaurant in the interior called El Capricho de Gaudí.

Gaudí widmete der Innenraumgestaltung des Wohnhauses besondere Aufmerksamkeit, und zwar sowohl im Hinblick auf die Aufteilung und Anordnung der Räume als auch auf die schmückenden Details. Auf diese Weise wurden den Bedürfnissen des Eigentümers, eines jungen ledigen Mannes, perfekt angepasste Räumlichkeiten entwickelt. Seit 1992 befindet sich das Gebäude im Besitz einer japanischen Unternehmergruppe, die hier das Restaurant El Capricho de Gaudí führt.

Large windows inundate the space with light. Another solution that visually enlarges the rooms is the high, coffered wood ceilings that are true works of art.

Großflächige Fenster durchfluten den Raum mit Licht. Die großzügige Deckenhöhe und die aufwändig gestalteten Holzvertäfelungen, die regelrechte Kunstwerke darstellen, sorgen für eine optische Vergrößerung der Räume.

The building's natural surroundings define its architectural profile. Tones borrowed from nature create harmonic chromatic contrasts.

Die Umgebung bestimmt das architektonische Profil des Bauwerks. Anleihen aus der Natur sorgen insbesondere bei der Farbgebung für harmonische Kontraste.

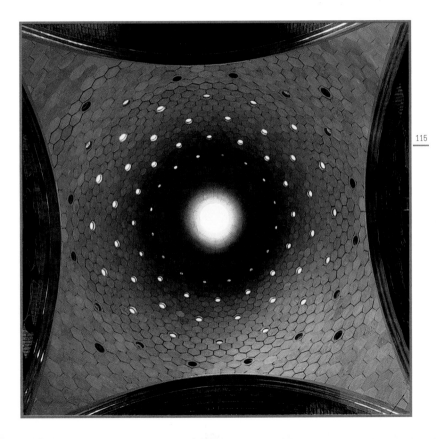

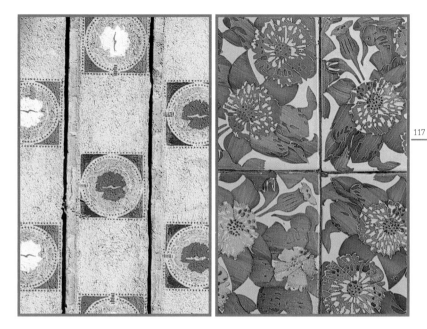

Gaudí resurrected the use of ceramics, another old decorative technique used in the Mediterranean zones. He managed to create surprising decorative images with tiles, starting with everyday and conventional elements.

Die Verwendung von Fliesen ist eine weitere in Vergessenheit geratene Technik zur Ausschmückung von Räumen und Gebäuden im Mittelmeerraum, die von Gaudí wiederentdeckt wurde. Durch den geschickten Einsatz von Kacheln erzielte er überraschende dekorative Effekte.

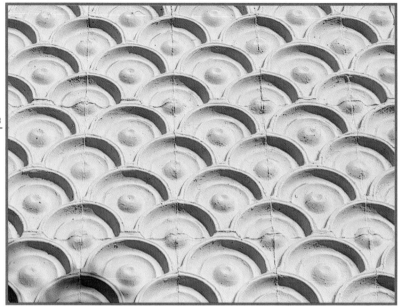

Gaudí combined the influence of historic tradition with ornamental ideas from other cultures. The Oriental and Islamic cultures frequently inspired his decorative finishes in which ceramics play an important role.

Gaudí verstand es, traditionelle Techniken und dekorative Elemente anderer Kulturen miteinander zu kombinieren. Oftmals ließ er sich dabei von Orient und Islam inspirieren – Kulturen, in denen Kacheln als schmückendes Element eine wichtige Rolle zukommt.

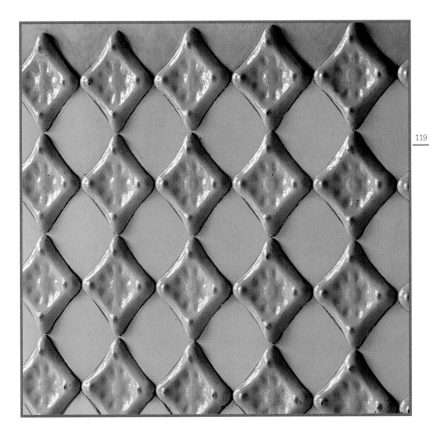

Eusebi Güell, one of Gaudí's best friends and the principal patron, commissioned the architect in 1884 to construct his estate between Les Corts and Sarrià, Barcelona neighborhoods that were then villages on the outskirts.

The vast plot of land incorporated three estates, Can Feliu and Baldiró Tower, acquired by Güell in 1870, and Can Cuyàs, purchased in 1883. The architect situated the main entrance of the palatial residence at the Cuyàs estate. This area includes two gates, one for people and another for carriages, and is flanked by two pavilions: the caretaker's dwelling and the stables, linked by the space used as a manège ring.

The caretaker's quarters were designed as a pavilion distributed in three volumes. The main one has an octagonal floor plan, while the two adjacent ones have a rectangular arrangement. The stables were conceived as a unitary space with a rectangular layout covered with parabolic arches and covered vaults. Thanks to the use of trapezoidal openings, this area enjoys a generous amount of light, accentuated by the white walls. Next to this nave is a small room with a quadrangular design and domed roof that was previously an exercise ring.

Between the caretaker's quarters and the stables is a large wrought-iron gate that features the sculpture of a dragon. The Vallet i Piqué workshop handcrafted the piece in 1885 from an imaginative design by Gaudí. Adjacent to the gate, a smaller door gives access to pedestrians. A parabolic arch covered by a molding with vegetable motifs gives shape to this entrance.

Eusebi Güell, einer der besten Freunde und Hauptmäzen Gaudís, beauftragte den Architekten 1884 mit dem Bau eines Anwesens zwischen Les Corts und Sarrià, Stadtviertel im heutigen Barcelona, die seinerzeit noch Dörfer außerhalb des Stadtgebiets waren.

Auf dem weitläufigen Gelände befanden sich drei Gebäude, Can Feliu und Torre Baldiró, die Güell 1870 erwarb, und Can Cuyàs, das er 1883 kaufte. Auf Letzterem errichtete Gaudí den Haupteingang, dem er auf Wunsch des Besitzers enorme Wichtigkeit zumaß. Er besteht aus zwei Eingangstoren – eines für Fußgänger und das andere für Kutschen – mit jeweils einem Pavillon auf beiden Seiten für den Pförtner und die Stallungen, die durch die Reithalle verbunden sind. Das Pförtnerhaus war als dreiteiliger Pavillon konzipiert: der Hauptteil mit achteckigem und die beiden angrenzenden Räume mit rechteckigem Grundriss. Die Stallungen wurden als einheitlicher Raum mit rechteckigem Grundriss, Parabolbögen und verputzten Gewölben gestaltet. Die trapezförmigen Öffnungen lassen großzügig Licht einfallen und sorgen, zusammen mit dem Weiß der Wände, für Helligkeit. Neben diesem Raum wurde eine kleine, viereckige, mit einer Kuppel bedeckte Reithalle erbaut.

Zwischen dem Pförtnerhaus und den Ställen befindet sich das große schmiedeeiserne Tor mit der Drachenskulptur: Es handelt sich um eine Arbeit aus der Werkstatt Vallet i Piqué, die 1885 nach einem Entwurf Gaudís gestaltet wurde. Neben diesem Tor liegt ein kleineres für Fußgänger. Ein mit Pflanzenmotiven bedeckter Parabolbogen gibt diesem Eingang seine Form.

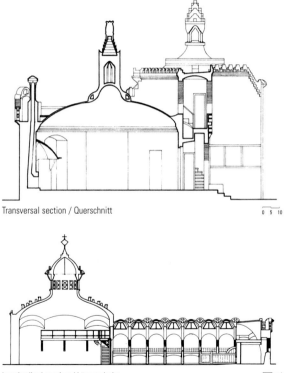

Transversal section / Querschnitt

0 5 10

Longitudinal section / Längsschnitt

0 1 2

Gaudí used new architectural languages and discovered vaulted forms that, over time, became common features of his work.

Gaudí bediente sich neuer architektonischer Ausdrucksformen. Er entdeckte die geschwungene Form, die sich mit der Zeit zu einer Konstanten in seinen Werken entwickelte.

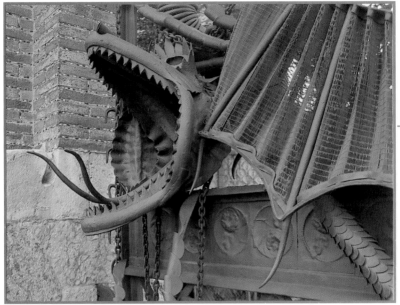

The Door of the Dragon, a masterly work of wrought iron, was inspired by Greek mythology. The dragon is both a decorative figure and the guardian who watches over the Gaudían universe hidden behind the gate.

Das Drachentor, eine meisterhafte Schmiedeeisenarbeit, ist von der griechischen Mythologie inspiriert. Der Drache ist nicht nur schmückende Figur, sondern auch Wächter des Gaudíschen Universums, das sich dahinter befindet.

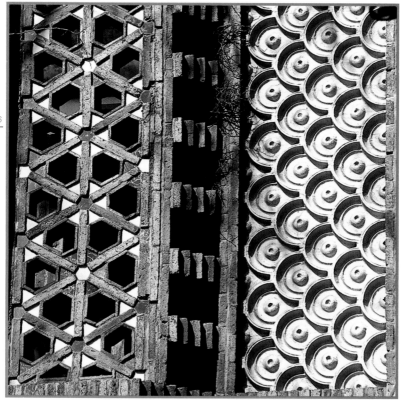

The dome that tops the stables is perforated by numerous openings in the form of windows that achieve a homogeneous illumination in the interior. The dome's covering of colorful ceramic pieces, as well as the finishing touch, a small tower of Moorish inspiration, create a certain baroque feeling that contrasts with the striking red brick and stone forms.

In die Kuppel über den Stallungen sind zahlreiche Fenster eingelassen, die den Innenraum gleichmäßig ausleuchten. Die Verkleidung dieser Kuppel sowie ihr eigentümlicher Abschluss erwecken einen beinahe barocken Eindruck, der in einem auffallenden Gegensatz zu den klaren Formen des Bauwerks aus rötlichem Ziegel und Stein steht.

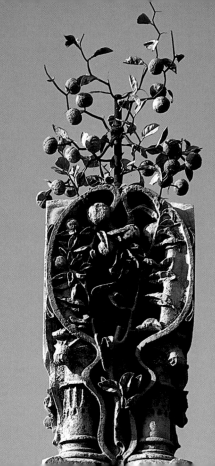

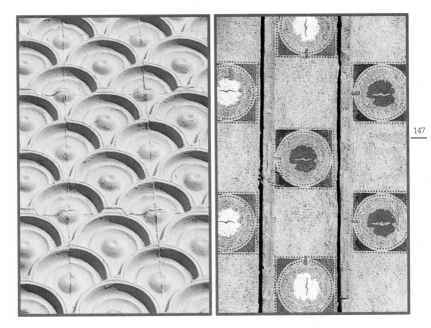

Gaudí unleashed his imagination and genius on the architectural and decorative resources used on the exterior and in the interior. Though the buildings have completely different styles, they are unified, in part, by the ornamental solution used to cover the façades of the stables and the caretaker's flat.

Gaudí ließ seinen Ideen und seinem Einfallsreichtum sowohl im Innenbereich als auch außen freien Lauf. Eine gewisse Einheitlichkeit in den stilistisch sehr unterschiedlichen Bauwerken erreicht er zum Teil durch eine verbindende Fassadendekoration.

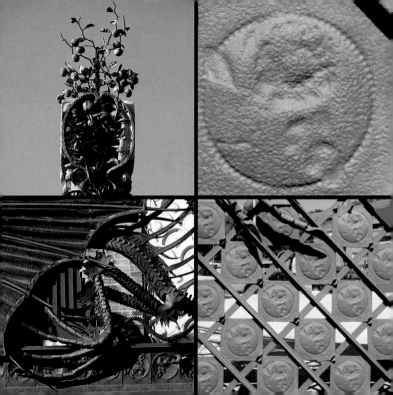

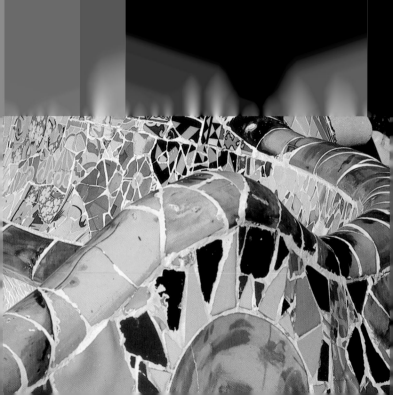

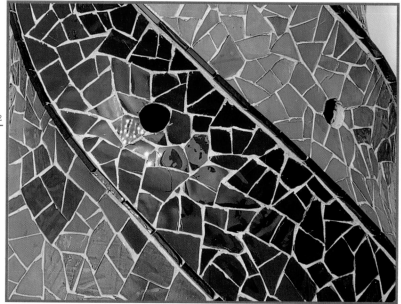

Gaudí covered surfaces with fragments of multi-colored ceramics, a decorative technique called *trencadís*. This solution, used for façades and different constructional details, is one of Gaudí's trademarks.

Gaudí verzierte die Oberflächen mit Kachelbruchstücken, einer Technik, die *trencadís* genannt wird. Dieses Gestaltungsmittel, an Fassaden und verschiedenen Details eingesetzt, wurde zu einem der Erkennungsmerkmale seines Stils.

Gaudí revived the old Mediterranean tradition of using broken tiles to decorate architectural elements. The application of trencadís also kept construction costs low.

Die Verwendung von Keramikbruchstücken für die Verkleidung der Oberflächen geht auf eine alte, von Gaudí wiederbelebte mediterrane Tradition zurück. Die Künstler kauften die Reste von den Kachelfabrikanten und konnten so gleichzeitig die Baukosten niedrig halten.

Temple Expiatori de la
Sagrada Família

1883-1926

In 1887, the congregation of devotees of Saint Joseph, led by the bookseller Josep Maria Bocabella, began the project of constructing a large expiatory temple. The architect Francisco de Paula del Villar, who offered to draw up the plans for free, designed a neo-Gothic church.

The first stone was put in place on March 19, 1882, the feast of Saint Joseph. Villar resigned as director one year later, after disagreements with the committee, whose chairman, Joan Martorell Montells, recommended that Gaudí, only 31 at the time, take charge of the construction. In 1884, Gaudí signed his first plans: the elevation and the section of the altar of the Chapel of Saint Joseph, which were inaugurated one year later.

Unlike Villar's neo-Gothic project, Gaudí imagined a church with numerous technical innovations, with a Latin cross superimposed over the initial crypt. Above it, the main altar was surrounded by seven domes. The doors of the crossing are dedicated to the Passion and the Nativity, and the principal façade to Glory. Above each façade, Gaudí designed four towers, twelve in total, which represent the Apostles, and in the middle one that symbolizes Jesus Christ, around which four more are dedicated to the Evangelists and one to the Virgin.

On June 12, 1926, Gaudí was run over by a tram and died three days later. He was buried in the crypt where he had spent the last years of his life. Since then, defenders and critics of the church have debated its completion, yet construction continues thanks to donations from around the world.

Im Jahr 1877 begannen Anhänger des heiligen Josef unter Führung des Buchhändlers Josep Maria Bocabella ihr Vorhaben, ein großes Gotteshaus zu bauen. Der Architekt Francisco de Paula del Villar, der sich anbot, die Pläne kostenlos anzufertigen, entwarf eine neugotische Kirche.

Der Grundstein wurde am 19. März 1882 gelegt; jedoch gab Villar die Leitung der Bauarbeiten ein Jahr später nach Auseinandersetzungen mit dem Ausschuss ab. Dessen Leiter, Joan Martorell, empfahl Gaudí, der mit nur 31 Jahren die Bauleitung übernahm. 1884 unterzeichnete er seine ersten Pläne: Aufriss und Detailansicht für den Altar der Kapelle des heiligen Josef, die ein Jahr später eingeweiht wurde.

Im Unterschied zu Villars neugotischem Entwurf stellte sich Gaudí eine Kirche mit vielen technischen Neuerungen vor, mit einem Grundriss in der Form eines lateinischen Kreuzes, das über die Krypta gelegt ist. Auf ihr wird der Hochaltar von sieben Kapellen umgeben. Die Tore des Kreuzschiffs wurden der Passion und der Geburt gewidmet und die Hauptfassade der Glorie. Über jeder Fassade waren vier Türme geplant, zwölf insgesamt, die die Apostel verkörpern. Mittig ein Turm, der Jesus Christus symbolisiert, vier weitere für die Evangelisten und einer für die Jungfrau Maria.

Am 10. Juni 1926 starb Gaudí. Er wurde in der Krypta beigesetzt, in der er die letzten Jahre seines Lebens verbracht hatte. Seither debattieren Befürworter und Gegner immer wieder über die Beendigung der Bauarbeiten; währenddessen werden die Arbeiten jedoch mithilfe von Spenden aus aller Welt weitergeführt.

Study of the temple / Skizze

Perspective / Perspektive

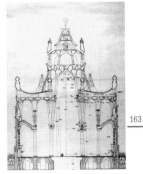

Section / Schnitt

0 3 6

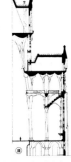

I   II   III

Evolution of the sections / Entwicklung der Schnitte

0 2 4

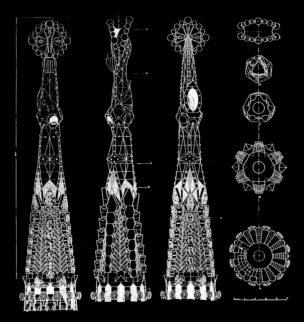

Elevations and sections of the towers

Aufrisse und Schnitte der Türme

Construction on the church has continued for more than a hundred years and the end is still far off.

Die Arbeiten an der Kirche gehen seit mehr als hundert Jahren ununterbrochen weiter, und ihr Ende liegt noch in weiter Ferne.

The Sagrada Família was begun
with stone from the quarry of
Montjuïc, but after its abandonment
in 1956, the work continued with
artificial stone and concrete.

Die Sagrada Família wurde anfangs
mit Gestein aus dem Steinbruch des
Montjuïc gebaut, seit 1956 jedoch
wird mit künstlichem Gestein und
Beton weitergearbeitet.

The lines of the internal part of the Façade of the Nativity are much more restrained than the lines of the exterior. The forms are austere, like those of Bodegas Güell; however in this case, they will be eventually accompanied by sculptures.

Das Innere der Geburtsfassade ist zurückhaltender als die Außenfassade. Die Formen sind wie die der Bodegas Güell asketisch, wobei sie in diesem Fall von Skulpturen begleitet werden.

The sculptures that the artist designed for the façades of the temple are based on life-size plaster, mock-ups that Gaudí modeled on people and live animals. A curious example is a Roman soldier from the Massacre of the Innocents, which he based on the waiter of a nearby tavern.

Die Skulpturen für die Fassaden wurden aus Gipsformen in naturgetreuem Maßstab hergestellt, die Gaudí am Vorbild lebendiger Menschen oder Tiere erarbeitete. Ein kurioses Beispiel hierfür ist das des römischen Soldaten bei der Enthauptung der unschuldigen Kinder, für den der Hilfskellner einer nahe gelegenen Taverne Modell stand.

Since it is difficult to replace the pieces that cover the spires of the towers, Gaudí commissioned workers from Murano, in Venice, to create vitreous pieces of mosaic, which are much more resistant.

Da es schwierig ist, die Turmspitzen zu ersetzen, bediente sich Gaudí hier wesentlich widerstandsfähigerer Materialien. Um die Spitzen der Türme abzudecken, gab er Elemente aus Glaskeramik in Murano bei Venedig in Auftrag.

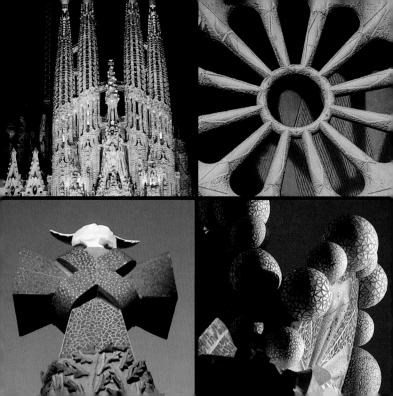

The architect's fervent faith and Catholic devotion greatly influenced his work. His projects became a religious exaltation and an expression of his strong nationalist feelings. The architect's beliefs are evident in buildings like the crypt of Colònia Güell and the Sagrada Família.

Der von dem Architekten intensiv gelebte katholische Glaube beeinflusste sein Schaffen sehr. Seine Entwürfe wurden zu Übertreibungen und Übersteigerungen seines ebenfalls ausgeprägten Nationalgefühls. Die Krypta der Colònia Güell, die Sagrada Família oder das Haus Bellesguard sind Beispiele hierfür.

Gaudí once said, "My soul is not in a hurry," when people asked him with impatience about works on the Sagrada Família. Gaudí consecrated his architecture and his life to God, and many of his works prove it.

„Meine Seele hat es nicht eilig", lautete Gaudís Antwort auf die ungeduldigen Nachfragen zur Fertigstellung der Sagrada Família. Das Genie widmete seine Architektur und sein Leben Gott, seine Bauten bezeugen dies.

Palau Güell

1886-1888

Declared a World Heritage site by UNESCO, Palau Güell, another assignment that Eusebi Güell awarded to his protégé, is the building that made Gaudí famous. The architect designed this residence without fear and with an unlimited budget. The employment of the best stones, the best ironwork, and the best cabinetry made this house the most expensive building of its time.

The peculiar location of this urban palace, on a narrow street in Barcelona's old quarter, makes it impossible to view the construction as a whole from the exterior. Güell decided to construct his residence on this street for two reasons: to make use of his family properties and to try to change the neighborhood's unfavorable image.

The sober and austere stone façade does little to warn the visitor of the majestic and opulent interior in which Gaudí displayed an unprecedented luxury. More than 25 designs preceded the definitive façade, which features forceful, historicist lines and a subtle classicism. Two large doors in the form of parabolic arches perforate the front and provide access for both carriages and pedestrians. The palace includes a basement, four floors, and a rooftop terrace.

For many years, the palace was a social, political, and cultural center. During the Civil War (1936–39), anarchists confiscated the residence and used it as a house for troops, and a prison. In 1945, it was acquired by the Diputación of Barcelona. Today, Palau Güell marks the beginning of the Modernist trail.

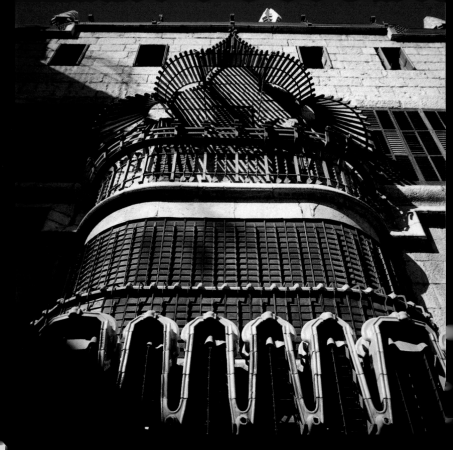

Von der UNESCO zum Weltkulturerbe erklärt, war der Palau Güell ein weiterer Auftrag von Eusebi Güell für seinen Protegé. Der Architekt entwarf diese Residenz sorglos mit unbegrenztem Budget. Es wurden die besten Steine, das beste Schmiedeeisen und die beste Tischlerarbeit eingesetzt und wurde so zum teuersten Gebäude jener Zeit.

Die Lage dieses Stadtpalais in einer engen Straße der Altstadt Barcelonas lässt es nicht zu, das Bauwerk von außen als Ganzes zu betrachten. Güell beschloss aus zwei Gründen, seinen Wohnsitz dort einzurichten: er wollte den Familienbesitz nicht aufgeben sowie den schlechten Ruf der Gegend verbessern.

Die nüchterne Fassade aus Stein lässt kaum den majestätischen Überfluss im Inneren des Hauses erahnen, das Gaudí mit unerhörtem Luxus ausstattete. Der endgültigen Fassade gingen 25 Vorentwürfe voran, und sie wurde mit ausdrucksstarken, historistischen Linien und subtilen klassischen Zügen verwirklicht. Zwei große Tore in Form von Parabolbögen gewähren Kutschen und Fußgängern Zugang zu dem Gebäude, das über einen Keller, vier Stockwerke und eine Dachterrasse verfügt.

Der Palast war einige Jahre ein gesellschaftliches, politisches und kulturelles Zentrum. Während des Bürgerkriegs (1936–39) wurde er von den Anarchisten besetzt und als Kaserne für die Truppen benutzt. Im Keller richtete man ein Gefängnis ein. 1945 erwarb die Provinzialverwaltung das Gebäude. Zurzeit ist der Palau Güell der Ausgangspunkt der Ruta del Modernismo.

The terrace roof is a distinctive element of Palau Güell and would later have an even more important role in the Pedrera. Using his imagination, Gaudí drew an imaginative rooftop with impossible forms. The volumes have a decorative and sculptural power, as well as a practical function, since they serve as chimneys and ventilation ducts for the building.

Im Palau Güell ist die Dachterrasse charakteristisches Merkmal, wie auch bei der Pedrera. Gaudí schafft einen märchenhaften Ort voller fantasievoller Figuren und Formen. Neben ihrem dekorativen Charakter besitzen diese Elemente praktische Funktionen, denn darunter verbergen sich die Schornsteine und Belüftungsrohre des Gebäudes.

In order to dress up these functional elements, Gaudí used brick for the chimneys and ventilation ducts connected to the service space and kitchen. To cover volumes coming from the areas used by the Güell family and their guests, Gaudí used *trencadís* (pieces of multi-colored tile).

Für die Verkleidung benutzte Gaudí einerseits Ziegelsteine für die Kamine und Belüftungsschächte zu den Räumen der Bediensteten und den Küchen und andererseits *trencadís* für die Schächte zu den herrschaftlichen Gemächern und den von der Familie Güell und ihren Gästen bewohnten Räumen.

Gaudí created a building that aroused astonishment and even rejection for its new constructional solutions.

Gaudí ließ ein Gebäude entstehen, das aufgrund seiner neuartigen Konstruktionslösungen gleichermaßen Erstaunen wie Ablehnung hervorrief.

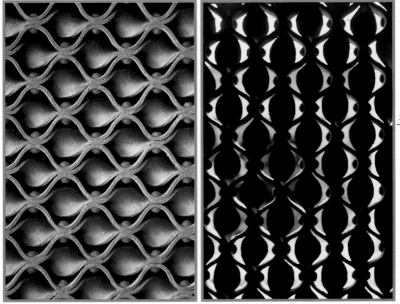

Gaudí constantly played with optical illusions and architectural solutions that tricked the visitor into believing that a space was larger than it actually was.

Gaudí spielte ständig mit optischen Täuschungen und architektonischen Lösungen, die den Besucher in die Irre führen und ihn glauben machen sollten, er befinde sich in einem Raum mit wesentlich großzügigeren Ausmaßen, als dieser tatsächlich hat.

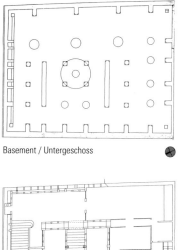

Basement / Untergeschoss

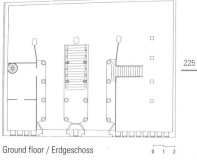

Ground floor / Erdgeschoss

0 1 2

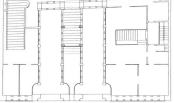

First floor / Erstes Obergeschoss

Second floor / Zweites Obergeschoss

0 1 2

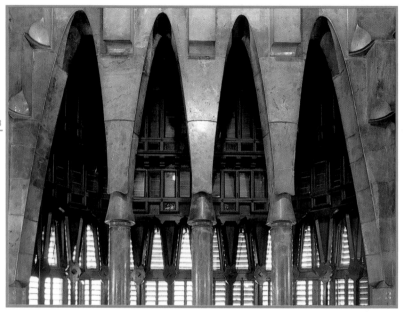

Gaudí found inspiration for the unique dome, which is designed like a starry sky inside the palace, at the dome of Hagia Sophia in Istanbul. The dome dominates the space and bathes the large central room in light.

Es war die Hagia Sophia in Istanbul, von der sich Gaudí beim Entwurf der fantastischen Kuppel inspirieren ließ. Die runden Löcher in der Kuppel sollen den Sternenhimmel darstellen; sie tauchen die Halle in ein einzigartiges Licht.

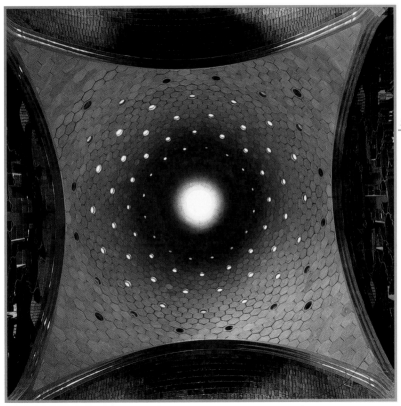

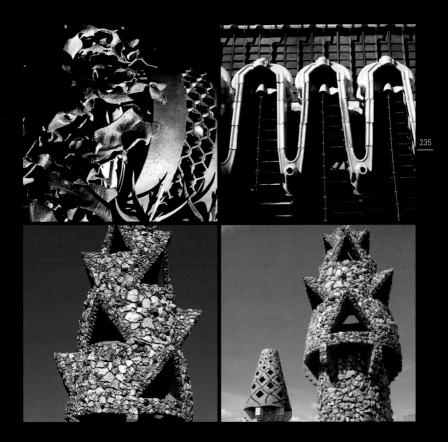

Palacio episcopal
de Astorga

1889-1893

After a devastating fire completely destroyed the episcopal palace of Astorga, Bishop Joan Baptista Grau i Vallespinós commissioned Gaudí to create a new episcopal seat. The relationship between the two had been formed years earlier, when Grau was vicar-general of the archdiocese of Tarragona and inaugurated the chapel of the College of Jesus and Mary in Reus, whose altar was designed by Gaudí.

The first proposals that Gaudí sent delighted Grau, but did not convince the architecture section of the Academy of San Fernando in Madrid, which oversaw all ecclesiastical projects. After various modifications, the committee approved Gaudí's project, nevertheless a heated debate continued, and after Grau's death, Gaudí abandoned the Astorga project. Gaudí constructed a building reminiscent of a medieval fortification, with numerous Gothic details. The building was surrounded by a trench to facilitate ventilation and illuminate the basement.

For the entrance, Gaudí envisioned a large foyer that would rise up to the roof, illuminated by skylights that would distribute light to all floors. However, the architect who succeeded Gaudí, Ricardo García Guereta, disregarded this solution and constructed a totally blind roof, which hindered light from shining throughout the building.

On the façades, Gaudí used granite from Bierzo. Its light color has a symbolic function because it blends with the clergy's clothing. The pointed arches on the façade are decorated with glazed ceramic pieces made in the neighboring village, Jiménez de Jamuz.

Nachdem ein verheerender Brand den Bischofspalast von Astorga komplett zerstört hatte, gab der Bischof Juan Bautista Grau i Vallespinós Antoni Gaudí den Auftrag zum Entwurf eines neuen Bischofssitzes. Die Beziehung zwischen den beiden reicht Jahre zurück, als Grau als Generalvikar der Erzdiözese von Tarragona die Kapelle des Jesus-und-María-Kollegs in Reus eingeweiht hatte. Die ersten von Gaudí geschickten Vorschläge entzückten Grau, überzeugten aber nicht die Architekturabteilung der Akademie San Fernando in Madrid, die sämtliche kirchlichen Bauarbeiten überwachte. Nach mehreren Änderungen wurde das Projekt schließlich angenommen, aber die Meinungsverschiedenheiten hielten an, und nach dem Tode Graus gab Gaudí die Arbeiten endgültig auf. Es wurde ein Gebäude errichtet, das mit vielen gotisch anmutenden Details an mittelalterliche Festungen erinnert. Das Bauwerk ist von einem Graben umgeben, um Belüftung und Beleuchtung des Untergeschosses zu ermöglichen.

Für den Eingang sah Gaudí eine große Empfangshalle vor, die bis zum Dach reichte und über einige Lichthöfe sämtliche Stockwerke erhellte. Der Nachfolger Gaudís, Ricardo García Guereta, errichtete jedoch ein vollkommen geschlossenes Dach, was sich ausgesprochen nachteilig auf die Lichtverhältnisse im gesamten Gebäude auswirkte.

Für die Fassaden wurde Bierzo-Granit verwendet, dessen helle Farbe eine symbolische Funktion hat, da sie den Gewändern der Geistlichen ähnelt. Die Streben der Spitzbögen wurden mit im Nachbardorf hergestellten Glaskeramiksteinchen verziert.

"In modern architecture, the Gothic style must be a starting point but never the ending point."

„In der modernen Architektur sollte die Gotik zwar einen Ausgangspunkt bilden, aber niemals den Endpunkt."

Gaudí completed the liturgical reformation in this large building made of granite from Bierzo.

Gaudí materialisierte die Reform der Liturgie in diesem großen Bauwerk aus Bierzo-Granit.

Gaudí's work on the cathedral of
Palma de Mallorca and the Sagrada
Família was based on the
architect's long conversations with
his friend, the Bishop of Astorga.

Gaudís Arbeiten an der Kathedrale
von Palma de Mallorca und der
Sagrada Família gehen auf lange
Gespräche mit dem Bischof von
Astorga zurück, mit dem er eng
befreundet war.

The pointed arches on the palace's ground floor are covered with small, dark red varnished ceramic pieces. The architect designed the templates and assigned Jiménez de Jamuz to create the ornaments. Gaudí did not design the floral engravings.

Die spitzbogigen Strebepfeiler im Erdgeschoss des Palastes sind mit kleinen dunkelrot glasierten Keramiksteinchen verkleidet. Der Architekt entwarf die Schablonen und beauftragte Jiménez de Jamuz mit den Ornamenten. Die floralen Gravuren in Gips stammen nicht von Gaudí.

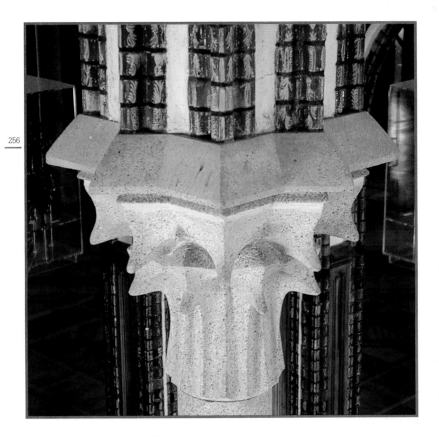

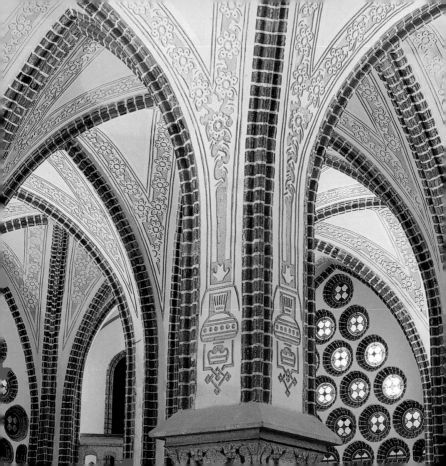

260

The cylindrical shaft columns that support the pointed arches are austere. Their capitals are adorned with subtle floral motifs and their bases are made of simple geometric forms that combine hexagons, small circles, and flat polyhedrons.

Die Säulen mit zylinderförmigem Schaft, die die Spitzbögen tragen, wirken streng, doch ihre Kapitelle sind mit Blumenmotiven verziert. Die Sockel bestehen aus einfachen, miteinander kombinierten geometrischen Formen: Sechsecke, kleine Kreise und flache Vielecke.

Col·legi de les
Teresianes

1888-1889

Several conditions, such as the rule of poverty followed by this Carmelite community and the fact that the building was dedicated to Saint Teresa, founder of this order, strongly influenced the design of this school located in the Sant Gervasi neighborhood of Barcelona.

Another architect oversaw the initial works of the site until Gaudí took over in March 1889, assuming that the first and second floors of the building had already been determined. Gaudí stayed within the budget for the project, which was limited in comparison with other projects, and also followed the principles set by the previous architect, including the austerity, asceticism, and sobriety that this ecclesiastical order required. Without abandoning his original and imaginative style, Gaudí exercised restraint and designed a building with striking yet restrained elements. Although absent in previous works, moderation plays a key role in this project. For the façade, Gaudí designed a rigorous volume of stone and brick which includes various ceramic ornamental elements.

On the ground floor two large interior patios distribute the natural light. Gaudí replaced the heavy transverse load-bearing walls, using parabolic arches with symmetrical hallways. This constructional solution eliminated the wall as a supporting element and created a dynamic composition. The arches, painted white to accentuate luminosity, are separated by windows that open on to the interior patios. The result is a tranquil atmosphere bathed in a soft, indirect light.

Einige Vorbedingungen prägten den Entwurf für das Colegio de las Teresianas, das sich im Stadtviertel Sant Gervasi von Barcelona befindet: das Armutsgelübde dieser Karmelitergemeinschaft und die Tatsache, dass das Gebäude der Ordensgründerin, der Heiligen Theresa, gewidmet werden sollte.

Ursprünglich leitete ein anderer Architekt das Projekt und Gaudí übernahm erst im März 1889 die Leitung. Das hatte zur Folge, dass der Grundriss bereits entschieden war und er das erste Stockwerk schon vollendet vorfand. Gaudí richtete sein Konzept nach dem Budget aus, das im Vergleich zu seinen anderen Aufträgen spärlich war. Er arbeitete nach den Vorgaben seines Vorgängers und entsprach mit seinem Entwurf den Anforderungen des Ordens, die Strenge und Schlichtheit vorsahen. Ohne seinen charakteristischen Stil aufzugeben, entwarf er ein Gebäude mit zurückhaltenden Linien. Der Umgang mit Materialien und Formen, auf den Gaudí in seinen vorangegangenen Arbeiten keine Rücksicht nehmen musste, stand hier im Vordergrund.

Gaudí wählte für die Außenfassade Ziegelstein mit wenigen dekorativen Keramikelementen. Die massiven tragenden Mauern ersetzte er durch Parabolbögen, die dem Ganzen eine starke Dynamik verliehen. Weißer Putz unterstreicht die Helligkeit der Flure. Das Ergebnis ist eine ruhige, von sanftem indirektem Licht getragene Atmosphäre.

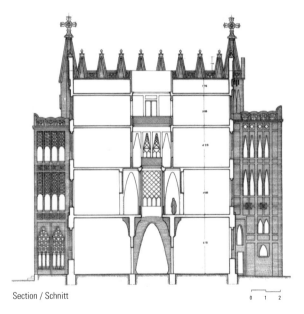

Section / Schnitt

0 1 2

The conception of this work, like many before it, is enormously organic and shows a clear Gothic inspiration. This is demonstrated by the wrought-iron work of the entrance door, which is repeated in some windows on the ground floor and on the second floor, as well as on the blinds and in the interior of the construction.

Das Konzept des Colegio de las Teresianas ist wie das vieler seiner anderen Gebäude von der Gotik inspiriert. Die schmiedeeiserne Arbeit der Eingangstür, die sich unter anderem in einigen Fenstern des Erdgeschosses und der zweiten Etage sowie an den Rolläden wiederholt, ist hierfür ebenso ein Beweis wie die Spitzbögen der Durchgänge und Fenster.

Inspired by the symbolism of the seven levels of the ascent of Saint Theresa of Ávila, Gaudí designed this construction whose forceful and pointed profile stands out from the surrounding buildings.

Beim Bau der Schule der Karmelitergemeinschaft ließ sich Gaudí von der Himmelfahrt der Heiligen Theresa anregen. Das ausdrucksstarke Bauwerk hebt sich deutlich von den angrenzenden Gebäuden ab.

"We didn't change; the more time we spent reflecting on new forms of architecture, the more certainty we had for the need to use them."

„Wir haben uns nicht verändert; je länger wir über die neuen architektonischen Formen nachdachten, desto sicherer waren wir, diese verwenden zu müssen."

Casa de
los Botines
1892-1893

While Gaudí was finishing the construction of the episcopal palace in Astorga, his friend and patron, Eusebi Güell, recommended him as the architect for a house in the center of León. Simón Fernández and Mariano Andrés, the owners of a company that bought fabrics from Güell, commissioned Gaudí to build a residential building with a warehouse. The nickname of the house comes from the last name of the company's former owner, Joan Homs i Botinàs.

The architect wanted to pay tribute to León's emblematic buildings. Therefore, he designed a building with a medieval air and numerous neo-Gothic characteristics.

The principal door is crowned by a wrought-iron inscription with the name of the company and a large sculpture by San Jorge. During the restoration of the building in 1950, workers discovered a lead tube under the sculpture containing the original plans signed by Gaudí, and press cuttings from the period.

On the ground floor, the architect for the first time used a system of cast-iron pillars that leave the space free, without the need for the load-bearing walls to distribute it. Unlike Gaudí's previous projects, the façades of Casa de los Botines have a structural function.

On the inclined roof, six skylights supported by iron tie-beams illuminate and ventilate the attic. The ensemble is supported on a complex wooden framework. In 1929, the savings bank of León bought the building and adapted it to its needs, without altering Gaudí's original concept. At present the building is occupied by Caja de España.

Während Gaudí noch die Arbeiten am Bischofspalast von Astorga beendete, empfahl ihn sein Freund und Mäzen Eusebi Güell für ein Projekt im Zentrum von León. Simón Fernández und Mariano Andrés, Besitzer eines Unternehmens, das bei Eusebi Güell Stoffe kaufte, beauftragten Gaudí mit dem Bau eines Wohnhauses mit Lager. Der Name des Hauses geht auf den ehemaligen Besitzer des Unternehmens, Joan Homs i Botinàs, zurück.

Der Architekt wollte sich an den charakteristischen Bauwerken Leóns orientieren und entwarf ein Gebäude mit mittelalterlichen Reminiszenzen und zahlreichen neugotischen Stilmitteln.

Die Haupteingangstür ist von einer schmiedeeisernen Inschrift mit dem Namen des Unternehmens und einer großen Skulptur des Heiligen Georg gekrönt, unter dem man während der Restaurierung 1950 eine Bleikapsel mit den von Gaudí unterzeichneten Originalplänen fand. Für das Erdgeschoss griff der Architekt erstmals auf ein System von gusseisernen Pfeilern zurück, sodass der vorhandene Raum nicht mehr durch tragende Mauern unterteilt wurde. Im Unterschied zu späteren Werken hatten die Fassaden immer noch eine stützende Funktion.

Auf dem Dach sorgen sechs von Eisenbalken getragene Oberlichter für Beleuchtung und Belüftung des Dachbodens. Der Komplex stützt sich auf ein Gerüst aus Holz über dem Balkenträger. 1929 kaufte die Sparkasse von León das Gebäude und passte es ihren Anforderungen an, ohne den Entwurf von Gaudí zu verändern. Derzeit beherbergt es die Caja de España.

In the corners of the house, Gaudí placed cylindrical towers topped with a column, which is doubled in height on the northern side to indicate the direction. Gaudí liked to show the cardinal points of the compass in his buildings and did so in Palau Güell, Bellesguard, Park Güell, and Casa Batlló.

An den Ecken des Hauses befinden sich Rundtürme mit doppelten Kapitell-Abschlüssen im Nordteil. Gaudí wies an seinen Bauten mit Vorliebe die Himmelsrichtungen aus. Man findet solche Hinweise auch am Palau Güell, in Bellesguard, im Park Güell und an der Casa Batlló.

It was a challenge for Gaudí to create a neo-Gothic work in the center of León, near the splendid cathedral. His project surpassed all expectations and respected the environment.

Die Errichtung eines neugotischen Bauwerks in der Nähe der beeindruckenden Kathedrale stellte eine große Herausforderung dar. Gaudí übertraf alle Erwartungen mit einem Gebäude, das sich perfekt seiner Umgebung anpasst.

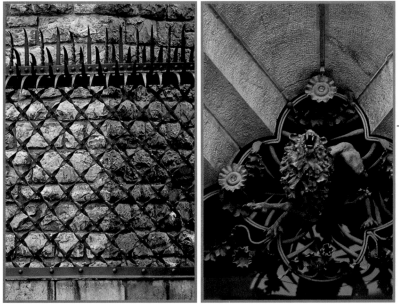

The interior, which has been totally remodeled over the years, still contains some of the elements designed by Gaudí, including the magnificent marquetry work in the doors and windows and wrought-iron elements such as the banisters and railings. In some rooms, one can still contemplate the original structure made of a system of metal pillars with stone capitals.

In dem über die Jahre hinweg mehrfach renovierten Inneren sind noch einige der von Gaudí entworfenen Elemente erhalten. Besonders eindrucksvoll sind die Intarsienarbeiten an Türen und Fenstern sowie die schmiedeeisernen Elemente an Geländern und Gittern. In einigen Räumen liegt die Konstruktion offen und zeigt ein System von Metallpfeilern mit Steinkapitellen.

The fascinating structure of the towers includes a framework of wooden strips with a helical form that are held up by vertical posts. Despite the irregularity of the pieces, the system is stable and has never required restoration.

Das faszinierende Fachwerk der Türme ist spiralförmig angelegt, senkrechte Stützpfeiler verbinden die Holzbänder miteinander. Trotz der ungleichmäßigen Beschaffenheit der einzelnen Teile ist der Komplex in sich stabil und musste bei den Instandsetzungsarbeiten nicht verstärkt werden.

Bodegas Güell

1895

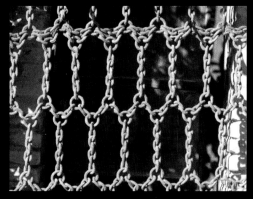

For many years, it was believed that the Bodegas Güell were designed by Francesc Berenguer i Mestres. However, the plans were not in the architect's archives and other factors led to the conclusion that Eusebi Güell had once again entrusted Gaudí to execute this project on one of his estates.

The land is located on the coast at Garraf, to the south of Barcelona. The development includes two buildings, an entrance pavilion and the bodegas. In front of the buildings is a large iron door formed by a crossbeam of wrought iron with thick chains hanging from it. A grand arch crowned by a glazed projecting balcony receives visitors and contains the door of the concierge's house.

The bodegas are located in an austere and striking building, evocative of military architecture and made of stone extracted from nearby quarries. The roof has two pitched elements, one of which reaches to the ground and becomes part of the façade. Experts say the architect was inspired by oriental pagodas. The chimneys are typical of Gaudí and display his surprising imagination.

The cellars are located on the ground floor. The first floor contains the residence, and the attic accommodates a chapel, which explains the appearance of a bell turret on the roof.

From a formal point of view, Bodegas Güell looks nothing like other buildings that Gaudí had, or would, design. However, the genius never repeated himself. His designs were a constant innovation in the fields of structure, composition, and construction. Thus it is not unusual that the resources used here were not repeated in other projects.

Viele Jahre lang vermutete man, die Bodegas Güell seien das Werk des Architekten Francesc Berenguer i Mestres. Da in dessen Archiv aber die Zeichnungen dazu fehlten, liegt die Schlussfolgerung nahe, dass Eusebi Güell die Durchführung wieder Gaudí anvertraute.

Das Gelände liegt südlich von Barcelona an der Küste des Garraf. Der Komplex besteht aus zwei Gebäuden, Eingangspavillon und Lagerkeller. Ersterer besteht aus einem großen Eisentor mit einem geschmiedeten Querbalken, von dem dicke Ketten herabhängen. Für die tragenden Mauern wurde Kalk- mit Ziegelstein kombiniert. Ein großer, von einem Balkon gekrönter Bogen empfängt Besucher und beherbergt die Türe des Pförtnerhauses. Die Bodegas sind in einem streng gestalteten Gebäude untergebracht, das an Militärarchitektur erinnert. Die Verlängerung der Südostfassade bildet eine der Seiten des Giebeldaches, weshalb man den Eindruck hat, dass sich Gaudí von orientalischen Pagoden inspirieren ließ. Eines der Elemente, das auf Gaudí als Urheber dieses Projektes verweist, sind die mit überraschendem Einfallsreichtum konzipierten Kamine. Im Erdgeschoss wurden Lagerkeller eingerichtet, im ersten Stock Wohnräume, und im Dachgeschoss befindet sich eine Kapelle, zu welcher auch der Glockenturm auf dem Dach gehört.

Die Anlage ähnelte weder Gaudís vorherigen Entwürfen noch seinen späteren: Das Genie wiederholte sich niemals, seine Gebäude wiesen immer wieder strukturelle und kompositorische Neuerungen auf, so ist es nicht verwunderlich, dass Gaudí die eingesetzten Mittel später nicht noch einmal verwendete.

The Bodegas Güell rise up forcefully in a unique setting that the architect respected by using local materials.

Die kraftvolle Architektur der Bodegas Güell erhebt sich aus einer einzigartigen Landschaft, der Gaudí dadurch Respekt zollte, dass er ausschließlich Baumaterial aus der Umgebung verarbeitete.

The Bodegas Güell are located on the land for which Gaudí had originally designed a hunting pavilion. Eusebi Güell requested the pavilion, but it was never built.

Dort, wo sich heute die Bodegas Güell (Weinkeller) befinden, sollte ursprünglich ein Jagdpavillon, Gaudís erstes Projekt für Eusebi Güell, entstehen. Er wurde jedoch niemals gebaut.

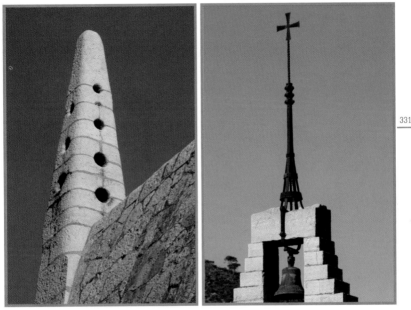

The building is located near the cave of the Falconera, where a large underground river flows into the sea. Güell wanted to divert the river towards Barcelona. In the grounds there is also a medieval watchtower that is connected to the residence via a bridge.

Das Gebäude befindet nahe der Falconera-Höhle, wo unterirdisch ein wasserreicher Fluss ins Meer mündet, den Güell nach Barcelona umleiten wollte. Auf dem Gelände gibt es auch einen mittelalterlichen Wachturm, der über eine Brücke mit den Wohngebäuden verbunden war.

The large roof that transforms into the façade emphasizes Gaudí's wish to link all the constructional elements of his works. The roof serves as an umbrella and a parasol for the building and has structural functions.

Das große Dach, das in die Fassade übergeht, unterstreicht Gaudís Bestreben, sämtliche Elemente in seinen Werken möglichst eng miteinander zu verbinden. So hat das Dach hier auch tragende Funktionen.

Casa Calvet

1898-1900

When Barcelona city council decided in 1900 to give an award for the best building of the year, officials chose the construction that Gaudí had designed for D. Pedro Martir Calvet. A textile manufacturer, Calvet commissioned the building from the architect in 1898. The award was the only recognition Gaudí received for a project during his lifetime. Casa Calvet was Gaudí's first attempt at residential housing design and represented a great challenge.

The Calvet building, located between party walls on a street in Barcelona's Eixample neighborhood, is one of Gaudí's most conventional constructions.

The owner reserved the main floor of the property for himself, as well as a warehouse and an office (now occupied by a restaurant) on the ground floor. Gaudí designed each one of the apartments in a different manner. The main façade, made of carved stone, displays more restrained forms than the rear façade, its apparent austerity contrasting with the creative foyer behind it. The extraordinary masonry work gives the building a rough aspect and a unique relief, which are softened by the lobed, wrought-iron balconies and diverse sculptural elements.

The architect gave special importance to the interior decoration of the residences. He designed some of the office furnishings, including the armchairs, a table, and a chair. The collection was his first foray into this area of design. He also created other decorative elements such as the ceilings, the peephole on the entrance door, the door handles and the ornamental pots in the back terrace.

Im Jahr 1900 verlieh die Stadtverwaltung von Barcelona den Preis für das beste Gebäude des Jahres dem von Gaudí 1898 für den Textilfabrikanten Pedro Martir Calvet entworfene Bauwerk. Diese Auszeichnung sollte die Einzige sein, die Gaudí zu Lebzeiten erfuhr. Die Arbeit war eine erste Annäherung an Entwürfe für nicht freistehende Häuser, eine große Herausforderung.

Die Casa Calvet, eingebettet zwischen Gebäuden in einer Straße des Eixample von Barcelona, ist wohl eines der konventionellsten Gebäude Gaudís.

Der Eigentümer behielt sich die Beletage vor sowie ein Lager und ein Büro (derzeit ein Restaurant) im Erdgeschoss. Gaudí entwarf jedes Stockwerk unterschiedlich. Die einheitliche Struktur der Hauptfassade wirkt durch die verwendeten Quadersteine rau und streng und steht der verspielten Eingangshalle gegenüber. Sie wird aber durch die geschwungenen, schmiedeeisernen Balkone und verschiedene Skulpturen aufgelockert.

Gaudí maß der Einrichtung der Wohnungen große Bedeutung bei. Er entwarf sogar einige Möbelstücke wie etwa Armsessel mit einem bzw. zwei Sitzen, einen Tisch und einen Stuhl. Diese Möbel stellten seinen ersten Versuch auf diesem Gebiet dar. Darüber hinaus gestaltete er Decken, das Fenster der Zugangstür, Türgriffe, Türklopfer und Blumentöpfe für die hintere Terrasse.

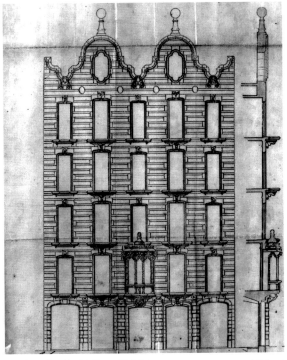

Elevation and section / Aufriss und Schnitt

0   1   2

Over the entrance door, which is placed exactly in the center of the main façade, is a small, lavishly decorated lookout platform. On the lower part is a crest of Catalonia, the owner's initial, and the image of a cypress. These are examples of symbolic references that would later have special significance in the Sagrada Família.

Über der Eingangstür – genau in der Mitte der Hauptfassade – ist ein reich verzierter kleiner Tribünenerker angebracht, in dessen unterem Teil das Wappen von Katalonien, die Initialen des Eigentümers und das Bild einer Zypresse dargestellt sind. All dies sind Beispiele für symbolische Anspielungen, die Gaudí später beim Bau der Sagrada Família bis ins letzte Detail ausfeilte.

"When the plasterers had to begin the ceilings, which were very ornate, they went on strike; so that the project would not be stalled and to teach them a lesson, I decided to substitute the suspended ceilings for simple wood panellings."

„Als die Stuckateure mit der Arbeit an den Decken beginnen sollten, für die ein reiches Dekor vorgesehen war, traten sie in Streik. Um eine Unterbrechung der Bauarbeiten zu verhindern und ihnen eine Lektion zu erteilen, beschloss ich, die Etagen stattdessen einfach mit dünnen Holzdecken auszustatten."

For the construction of this building, Gaudí opted to make a plaster model of the façade. He presented this solution, more practical, schematic, and detailed than blueprints, to City Hall. The consortium selected the building, by majority, not unanimously, as the best of the year.

Für den Bau dieses Hauses ließ Gaudí ein Gipsmodell der Fassade anfertigen. Diese Lösung war nicht nur praktischer, sondern auch genauer als die Zeichnungen, die er nur deshalb anfertigte, um sie der Stadtverwaltung vorzulegen. Der Gemeinderat wählte den Bau 1900 zum besten des Jahres.

For this building of rental apartments, Gaudí dared to freely interpret neo-Baroque, combining it with other, more personal styles.

Gaudí wagte sich an eine freie Interpretation des Neobarock, indem er diesen beim Entwurf für das Mietshaus – zweifellos eines seiner konventionellsten Werke – mit anderen, persönlicheren Stilen kombinierte.

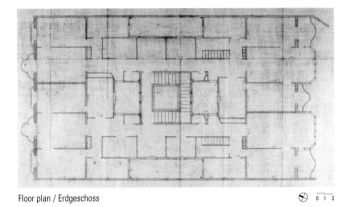

Floor plan / Erdgeschoss

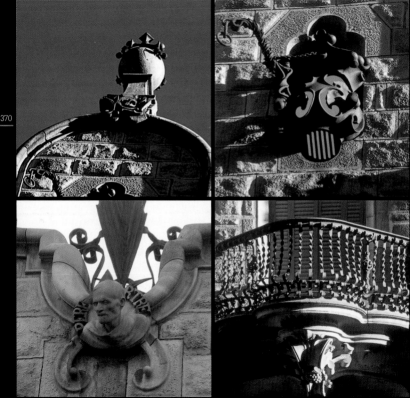

Furniture / Möbel

Gaudí's imagination was always filtered through a pronounced rationalism and a deep knowledge of architectural norms. His work in the field of furniture design also featured this double virtue: functionality and originality.

The need to be fully involved in his projects and the pleasure of design inspired him to create furnishings and numerous decorative elements.

His furniture, featuring solid forms and simple profiles, revived the definitive lines of medieval furnishings, while displaying the lively, sinuous and zigzag lines that are his trademark.

Gaudí tended to mix styles, which gave his furnishings a personal touch and a sculptural feel. Created in an artisan manner, his furniture combined ergonomics with beautiful and well-defined lines, often inspired by organic forms.

Das Bedürfnis Gaudís, in jedem seiner Werke ganz und gar aufzugehen, sowie seine Lust am Gestalten ließen den Architekten auch Möbelstücke und zahlreiche Elemente für Innen- und Außendekoration wie Türen, Gucklöcher, Türgriffe, Halter für Blumentöpfe, Lampen, Gitter, Balkone und vieles mehr erschaffen.

Seine Möbel weisen kräftige Formen und einfache Profile auf. In gewisser Weise greifen sie auf die einfachen Linien mittelalterlicher Möbel zurück und verbinden sie mit den für Gaudí so charakteristischen Zickzacklinien und lebendigen, geschwungenen Formen. Die von Gaudí gern verwendete Stilmischung drückte seinen an Skulpturen erinnernden Stücken ein persönliches Siegel auf. Alle Möbel sind handgefertigt und vereinen Ergonomie harmonisch mit schönen, klar umrissenen Linien, die meist von organischen Formen inspiriert sind.

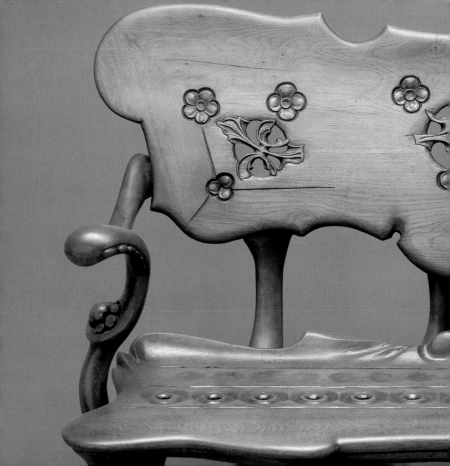

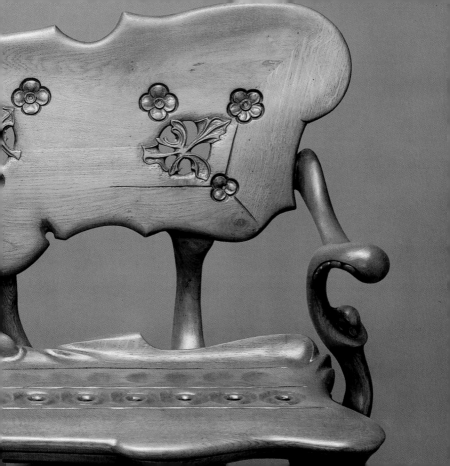

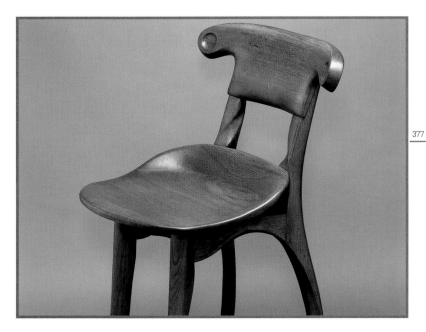

These chairs, made of carved and polished oak wood, were designed for Casa Calvet and Casa Batlló.

Der Architekt entwarf diese Stühle aus poliertem Eichenholz für die Casa Calvet und die Casa Batlló.

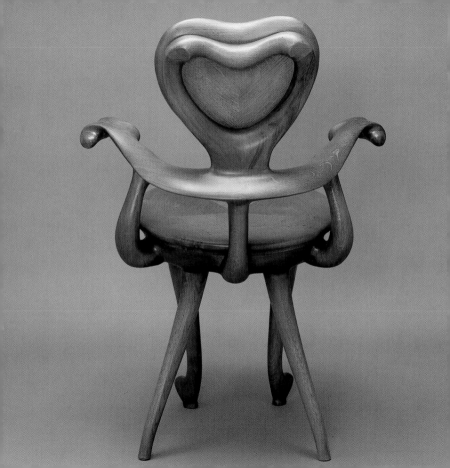

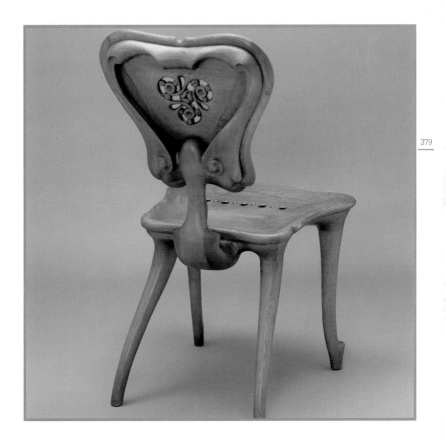

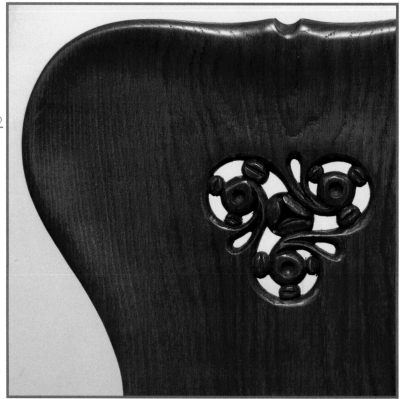

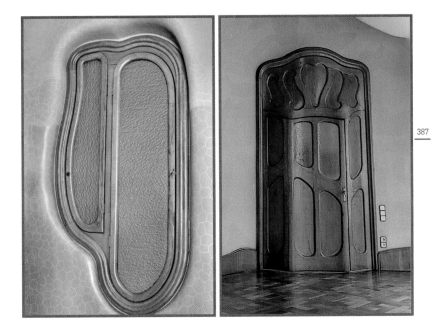

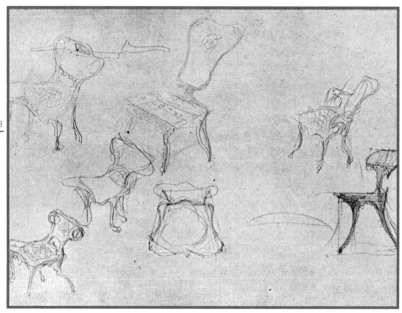

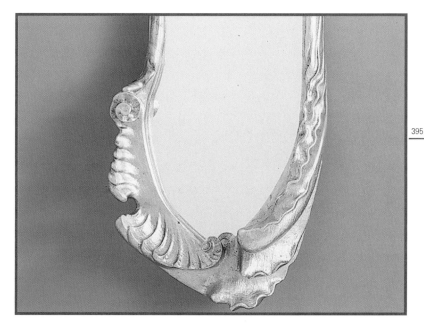

The shape of the mirror that Gaudí designed for Casa Calvet, made out of oak wood, achieves a balance between the neo-Baroque aesthetic and simple lines.

Die Form des Rahmens für diesen Spiegel in der Casa Calvet, in Eichenholz ausgeführt, verdeutlicht erneut das beeindruckende Gleichgewicht, das Gaudí zwischen neo-barocker Ästhetik und Schlichtheit herzustellen vermochte.

Stained glass windows

Buntglasfenster

The possibility of manufacturing thicker glass in different colors encouraged the use of stained-glass windows. As ornamentation, vegetable elements and polychromes dominate and manage to bathe the interiors with a variable and peculiar light.

Die Möglichkeit, auch stärkeres Glas in verschiedenen Farben herzustellen, veranlasste Gaudí, zunehmend Buntglasfenster einzusetzen. Farbigkeit und pflanzliche Elemente dominieren dabei und tauchen die Räume in ein wechselndes, besonderes Licht.

Stained-glass windows are an important element in Gaudí's work. The windows reaffirm the Modernist effort to integrate the arts into the functional aspects of architecture and to revive artistic traditions that had faded over the years.

Buntglasfenster spielen eine wichtige Rolle in Gaudís Entwürfen. Sie unterstreichen die moderne Idee, die Funktionalität der Architektur mit Elementen anderer Künste zu verbinden und gleichzeitig handwerkliche Traditionen wieder aufleben zu lassen, die im Laufe der Jahre verlorengegangen waren.

The Colonia Güell is one of Gaudí's most original and interesting works, even though the project was never completed. Construction began in 1908, but when Count Güell died in 1914, the project was abandoned. The assignment entailed a housing development for a small settlement of workers next to Eusebi Güell's textile factory in Santa Coloma de Cervelló, 20 kilometers from Barcelona, in Baix Llobregat.

An inspired Gaudí designed a complex settlement with constant references to nature. Gaudí's plan was to use organic forms and a studied polychromy so that the dark tones of the crypt's bricks would merge with the tree trunks, and the church walls would fuse with the green tone of the trees and transformed into blue and white in order to blend with the sky and the clouds. For Gaudí, this special chromatic plan represented nature and symbolized, at a deeper level, the path of the Christian life. Even though there are finished outlines, sketches, and even a model of the construction, Gaudí was only able to build the crypt, which can be considered as a small fragment of a majestic project.

The crypt is a complex and perfect skeleton made out of brick, stone, and blocks of basalt. Its floor plan has the shape of a star, made possible by the inclination of the exterior walls. Since the crypt is covered by a vault walled up with long, thin bricks on ribs of brick, it looks like the shell of a tortoise from the outside. Inside, it appears more like the enormous twisted skeleton of a snake. Four inclined columns of basalt situated at the entrance invite visitors to enter.

Die Colònia Güell ist eines der originellsten und interessantesten Werke Gaudís. Sie blieb unvollendet. Die Bauarbeiten begannen im Jahr 1908 und wurden nach dem Tod des Grafen Güell im Jahre 1917 eingestellt. Das Gotteshaus sollte inmitten einer Arbeitersiedlung entstehen, die ungefähr 20 Kilometer von Barcelona entfernt in Santa Coloma de Cervelló (Baix Llobregat) neben der Textilfabrik Eusebi Güells lag.

Gaudí entwarf eine Anlage mit Bezügen zur Natur. Die Kirche sollte mit der natürlichen Umgebung verschmelzen. Er verwendete organische Formen und eine abgestufte Farbigkeit. Die dunklen Töne der Steine in der Krypta sind Baumstämmen nachempfunden. Die Kirchenmauern in Grüntönen sollten sich mit der Farbe der Bäume vermischen, dann in Weiß oder Blau übergehen, um mit dem Himmel und den Wolken zu verschmelzen. Gaudí stellte die Natur dar und symbolisierte den Weg des christlichen Lebens. Die Entwürfe, Zeichnungen und das Modell des Werkes sind noch erhalten, aber nur die Krypta wurde gebaut, ein Bruchteil des majestätisches Werkes, ein komplexes Skelett aus Ziegel-, Naturstein und Basaltblöcken. Die Krypta ist wegen der Neigung der Außenmauern sternförmig. Die mit Ziegelsteinen verkleidete, von Ziegelsteinstreben getragene Wölbung erinnert von außen an den Panzer einer Schildkröte und von innen an das Skelett einer Schlange. Vier geneigte Basaltsäulen laden den Besucher zum Betreten des Raumes ein, der mit drei von Jujol entworfenen Altären ausgestattet ist.

Sketch of the crypt / *Skizze der Krypta*

Gaudí always placed great
importance on the non-architectural
elements of his works, such as the
furnishings.

Kennzeichnend für Gaudís
Architektur ist, neben den Aspekten
der Konstruktion und Liturgie, auch
anderen Elementen wie Möbeln
Wichtigkeit zu verleihen.

The large stained glass windows in resplendent colors, which perforate the crypt's walls, allow exterior light to enter, creating a spectacular play of light and shadow.

Die großzügigen Glasfenster in leuchtenden Farben, die die Mauer der Krypta durchbrechen, gestatten den Lichteinfall von außen und schaffen im Inneren ein abwechslungsreiches Spiel von Licht und Schatten.

Bellesguard

1900-1909

The country house of Maria Sagués, widow of Jaume Figueras and a fervent admirer of Gaudí, was the site of the 15th-century summer residence of the last Catalan king, Martí I ("The Human"). The name of the estate, Bellesguard, means "beautiful view." Dating from the Middle Ages, it refers to the estate's striking location and the splendid view of Barcelona. When Gaudí accepted the commission to design Maria Sagués' home, only few traces remained of what was formerly the medieval mansion of a king. The few remaining ruins were conserved.

The exterior the building, covered with stone, is reminiscent of medieval constructions and adapts to its surroundings. The various windows that perforate the walls of the façade are lobed arches in the Gothic style. The thin and graceful tower situated at one of the extremes of the residence features one of the architect's most characteristic elements: the four-pointed cross.

Bellesguard is a residence with a simple, practically square floor plan that includes a semi-basement, a ground floor, an apartment, and an attic. Covered vaults with low profiles supported by cylindrical pillars define the structure of the semi-basement. On the upper level, the brick vaults are decorative. In this space, great luminosity is achieved, thanks in part to the ample openings. On the upper floors, Gaudí created airy spaces by adding numerous windows and covering the walls with plaster. The roof of the attic is supported by a structure formed by mushroom-shaped capitals made of projecting brick. The capitals hold up a flat, partitioned panel out of which emerge false arches made of alternating thick bricks and tiles

Das Landhaus von Doña María Sagués, Witwe von Jaume Figueras und treue Anhängerin Gaudís, wurde auf dem Grundstück gebaut, wo im 15. Jahrhundert die Sommerresidenz von Martí I. l'Humà, des letzten Königs von Katalonien und Aragon stand. Der Name Bellesguard („schöne Aussicht") spielt auf die Lage mit einem großartigen Blick auf die Stadt an. Als Gaudí den Auftrag annahm, waren kaum Überreste des mittelalterlichen Landsitzes vorhanden. Gaudí respektierte die wenigen erhaltenen Ruinen.

Das Gebäude, mit schieferartigem Stein verkleidet, erinnert an mittelalterliche Bauten und passt sich in die Umgebung ein. Die Fenster haben gotisch anmutenden Bögen, und der Turm trägt ein Markenzeichen des Architekten, das vierarmige Kreuz.

Die Residenz ist auf einem einfachen quadratischen Grundriss erbaut und gliedert sich in Zwischengeschoss, Erdgeschoss, Wohnung und Dachgeschoss. Gipsverputzte, von zylindrischen Pfeilern getragene Gewölbe mit niedrigem Profil bestimmen die Struktur des Zwischengeschosses. Das Obergeschoss mit einem Gewölbe aus Ziegelstein ist dekorativer und dank breiter Durchbrüche sehr hell. In den oberen Stockwerken strukturierte Gaudí die Räume durch den Einsatz zahlreicher Öffnungen und den Gipsputz an den Wänden. Die Decke des Dachgeschosses wird von Pfeilern verschiedener Ausprägung mit pilzförmigen Kapitellen aus auskragenden Ziegelsteinen getragen. Auf diesen ruht eine verschalte Platte, von der falsche Bögen aus dünnen und dicken Ziegelsteinen ausgehen.

Gaudí abandoned the construction of Bellesguard in 1909, precisely 500 years after the date on which King Martí I married Margarida de Prades at the estate. Years later, the architect Domènec Sugrañes finished the project.

Im Jahre 1909, am 500. Jahrestag der Vermählung von Martí I. mit Margarida de Prades an diesem Ort, gab Gaudí das Projekt auf, und die Abschlussarbeiten wurden dem Architekten Domènec Sugrañes anvertraut.

Crowning the svelte and high tower of the building are the four-pointed cross, the royal crown, and the four bars of the Catalan-Aragonese flag. All of these elements are represented helically in stone and are covered with *trencadís*.

Das vierarmige Kreuz, die königliche Krone und die vier Streifen der katalanisch-aragonesischen Flagge krönen den hohen, schlanken Turm. All diese Elemente sind spiralförmig in Stein umgesetzt und mit Keramikscherben (*trencadís*) verkleidet.

Contrasting textures are habitual in the work of the Catalan architect and Bellesguard is no exception. Gaudí covered some windows with gratings; in this case, round iron bars. The gratings are a decorative element that, of course, also provide protection.

Materialkontraste sind im Werk des katalanischen Architekten üblich, und Bellesguard bildet hier keine Ausnahme. Gaudí bedeckt einige Fenster mit Gittern, in diesem Fall aus runden Eisenstäben. Dieses Element wird nicht nur als dekorative Lösung eingesetzt, sondern dient auch dem Schutz des Gebäudes.

Bellesguard is built on the same terrain on which King Marti l'Humà I constructed a retreat. The property has a view of the sea and the king could watch the galleys arrive. The estate is Gaudí's most significant tribute to Catalonia's great medieval past.

Gaudí versuchte, sich in jedem seiner Werke selbst zu finden. Steigt man zu den drei Kreuzen im Park Güell auf und stellt sich neben das Hauptkreuz, fällt der Blick auf das Bellesguard beherrschende vierarmige Kreuz.

The mosaics found in different spaces of the building are more than just decorative elements and should be interpreted as symbolic references to historic eras during which Catalonia enjoyed great political and economic splendor.

Die Mosaike müssen als symbolische Bezüge zu den Epochen der Geschichte gesehen werden, in denen Katalonien großen politischen und wirtschaftlichen Einfluss hatte.

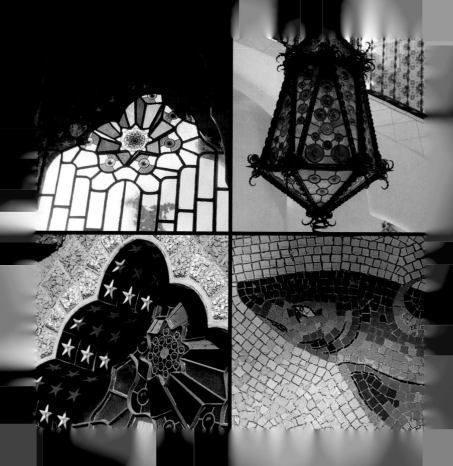

Park Güell

1900-1914

Eusebi Güell, an admirer of English landscape gardening, envisioned a new model of the English "garden city" when he decided to develop some land in the neighborhood of Gràcia known as the "Bald Mountain." Güell entrusted the project to his friend and protégé Gaudí, with the intention of creating a residential space near the city that would attract the wealthy Catalan bourgeoisie. It was an unsuccessful plan, and the terrain was converted into a public park in 1922, when Barcelona's City Hall bought the land from Güell's heirs.

Gaudí designed Park Güell as a housing development protected and isolated by a surrounding wall. With seven gates and undulating lines, the wall is made of rubble, with inlaid *trencadís* ceramics. The site was divided into 60 triangular parcels in order to adapt to the topography of the land, full of uneven stretches and slopes. Only three of the tracts were sold, however, one of which was purchased by Gaudí, where he lived before settling in the Sagrada Família. It now houses the Museu Gaudí.

The main door was originally located on Carrer Olot. Inside, two pavilions are designated for services and the concierge's residence. Both pavilions have an oval floor plan and display a notable absence of right angles. In front of this entrance, a grand double staircase leads to the Column Room and the Greek theatre. The flights of stairs are separated by small islands with organic decorative elements: a cave, a reptile head projecting out of a medallion with the Catalan flag, and the figure of a dragon.

Eusebi Güell, Bewunderer englischer Landschaftsgärten, dachte an das neue Modell der englischen Gartenstadt, als er beschloss, ein Gelände mit dem Namen Muntanya Pelada im Stadtviertel Gràcia zu bebauen. Den Auftrag gab er Gaudí mit der Absicht, ein Wohnviertel in Stadtnähe zu schaffen, das das gehobene katalanische Bürgertum anziehen sollte. Es erzielte allerdings nicht das erhoffte Interesse. Die Anlage wurde zu einem öffentlichen Park erklärt, als die Stadtverwaltung sie 1922 den Erben Güells abkaufte.

Gaudí plante das Gelände als abgeschlossene Siedlung, deshalb war es von Anfang an von einer Mauer umgeben. Diese mit sieben Eingangstoren versehene geschwungene Mauer ist mit *trencadís* verziert. Das Gelände wurde in 60 dreieckige Parzellen unterteilt und so dem von großen Höhenunterschieden und Abhängen geprägten Untergrund angepasst. Allerdings wurden nur drei Parzellen verkauft; eine kaufte Gaudí selbst, der dort wohnte, bis er in die Sagrada Família umzog. Heute beherbergt sie das Museo Gaudí.

Das Haupttor befand sich ursprünglich in der Carrer Olot. Dort befinden sich noch heute zwei Pavillons mit ovalem Grundriss, die als Personalunterkunft und Pförtnerwohnhaus dienten. Sie sind besonders geprägt durch das Fehlen jeglicher rechter Winkel. Gegenüber dem Eingang führt eine große doppelte Freitreppe zur Säulenhalle und zum griechischen Theater. Die Absätze der Treppe sind durch Inseln mit organischen dekorativen Elementen getrennt: eine Grotte, ein Reptilkopf, der aus einem Medaillon mit der katalanischen Flagge hervorragt, und die Figur eines Drachen.

Only on rare occasions has an architect managed to combine so brilliantly urbanism, architecture, and nature. Gaudí meticulously and skillfully created a fascinating space full of symbolism.

Nur sehr selten gelingt es, Städtebau, Architektur und Natur auf so meisterhafte Weise unter einen Hut zu bringen. Gaudí hat hier einen faszinierenden, überwältigenden Ort voller Symbolik geschaffen.

The pavilions that flank the door of the main entrance appear like something out of a fairy tale and entice the visitor to enter a magical world. The pavilions are made of stone, as is the wall that surrounds the property, and are covered with multi-colored *trencadís*. Though it doesn't seem so at first, the two buildings are perfectly integrated with the rest of Gaudí's composition.

Die märchenhaften Pavillons zu beiden Seiten des Haupteingangstores entführen den Besucher in eine magische Welt. Sie sind wie die Umfassungsmauer aus Stein und mit farbigen *trencadís* belegt, sodass sie sich harmonisch in das Gesamtkonzept der Anlage einfügen.

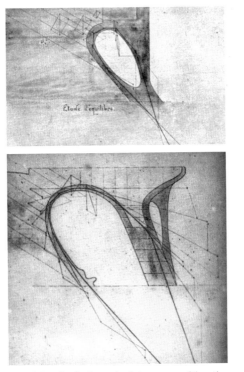

Study of the arches for the arcades that cover some of the paths.

Skizze für die Bögen, die einige der Wege überspannen.

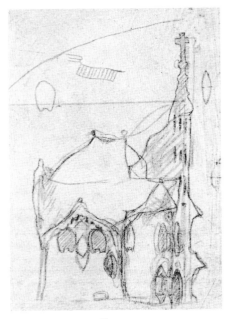

Sketch of the entrance pavilion.

Skizze des Eingangspavillons.

Cross that crowns one of the pavilions.

Kreuz als Abschluss eines der Pavillons.

Park Güell is the result of Gaudí's respect for the land and nature, his profound command of construction expertise, and his unlimited imagination.

Großer Respekt vor der Umgebung und der Natur, eine genaue Kenntnis baumeisterlichen Wissens und eine grenzenlose Vorstellungsgabe bringen das märchenhafte Szenario hervor, das der Park Güell darstellt.

With genius and determination, Gaudí designed the park as a residential paradise in the middle of the city, but it eventually became an urban park enjoyed by all of Barcelona.

Mit Genialität und Entschlossenheit schuf Gaudí eine Wohnstadt. Mit der Zeit verwandelte sich das, was ein bewohntes Paradies mitten in der Stadt sein sollte, in einen wunderbaren Park, der allen Bewohnern von Barcelona zur Verfügung steht.

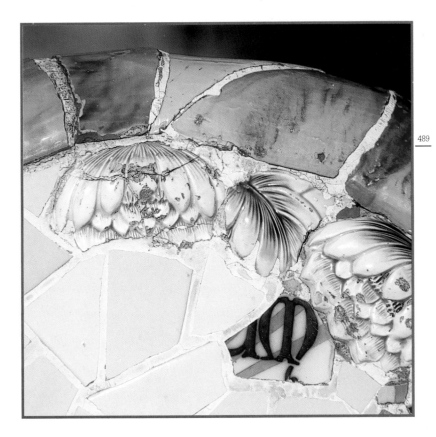

490

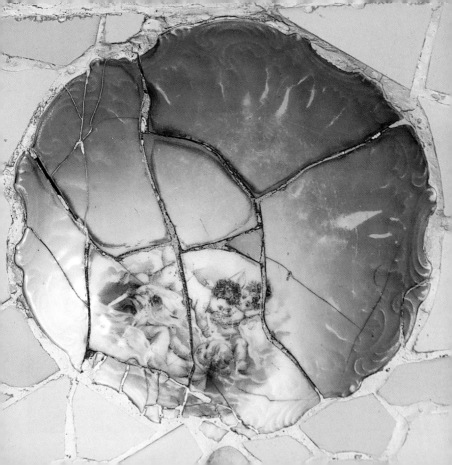

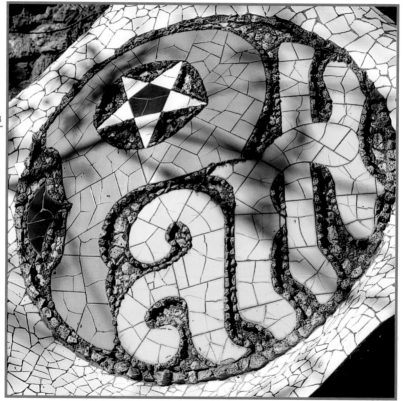

497

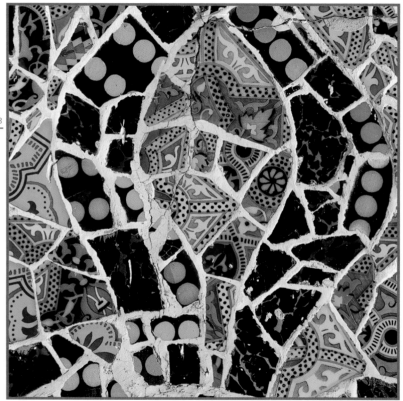

Stone's solidity and austerity contrasts with the richness and chromatic diversity of *trencadís*, which is used on the long, undulating bench situated on the esplanade overlooking the city, above the Column Room. Mosaic medallions adorn the Column Room's ceiling, the roof of the two pavilions, the steps and the entrance fountain.

Die Schlichtheit des Steins steht im Gegensatz zu der reichen Farben- und Formenpracht der *trencadís* der geschwungenen Bank, die die ganze Freiterrasse über der Säulenhalle einfasst, der Mosaikmedaillons, die ihre Decke schmücken, des Daches der beiden Pavillons oder der Freitreppe und des Springbrunnens am Eingang.

Gaudí's special creative universe included animal representations. Some of them were quite realistic, to the point of perfection. Others were born from fantasy, as animated beings that emerged from the artist's imagination.

Gaudís Originalität drückt sich auch in den vielfältigen Tiergestalten aus, die seinem kreativen Universum entsprungen sind. Einige sind sehr realistisch, andere sind als Fabelwesen auf die Welt gekommen und bezeugen die unermessliche Fantasie ihres Schöpfers.

The architect was a great observer of nature. His work is full of figures that represent animal forms. The use of animals in his architecture enlivens the constructions.

Der Architekt war ein hervorragender Beobachter der Natur. Sein Werk ist voller Tierfiguren, die den Bauwerken Leben verleihen.

Finca Miralles

1901-1902

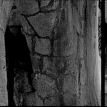

While Gaudí was immersed in his first grand residential project, Casa Calvet, he accepted another smaller assignment. His friend Hermenegild Miralles Anglès asked him to design a door and surrounding wall for his estate on Eusebi Güell's old private road. Today, the road is a busy avenue between the neighborhoods of Les Corts and Sarrià.

The materials Gaudí employed were ceramic bricks and the remains of Moorish tiles together with lime mortar. He crowned the wall with a continuous element that winds above the entire complex.

The entrance door has an irregular arched form. The wall opens to create access and folds through various curves. A helical interior framework of variable thickness supports the door, which seems to stand as if by magic, since there is no external element that absorbs the eccentric loads. A canopy completes the undulating forms of the entrance. It is formed by tie-beams built into the door, supported by fiber-cement tiles and helical braces. This element was eliminated in 1965 for exceeding municipal ordinances and was replaced by a smaller one in 1977.

To the right of the grand entrance, separated by a robust column with sinuous forms, is a small iron door that provides access to pedestrians. The lavish ironwork is particularly remarkable, given that the little flexible material was bent at its weakest point.

Während Antoni Gaudí mit seinem ersten Projekt für ein Wohnhaus, der Casa Calvet, beschäftigt war, nahm er einen weiteren Auftrag an. Sein Freund Hermenegild Miralles Anglès bat ihn um einen Entwurf für ein Tor und eine Umfassungsmauer für sein Haus an der alten Zugangsstraße zur Finca Güell (heute eine verkehrsreiche Straße zwischen den Stadtvierteln Les Corts und Sarrià). Als Baumaterial benutzte Gaudí Keramikziegel und Reste von arabischen Ziegeln, die mit Kalkmörtel abgebunden wurden. Ein durchgängiges schlangenförmiges Band windet sich als Abdeckung über die gesamte Länge der Mauer.

Das Einfahrtstor für Fahrzeuge hat eine geschwungene Form. Zur Gestaltung des Durchlasses öffnet und biegt sich die Mauer in verschiedenen Kurven. Das Tor scheint wie von Zauberhand aufrecht gehalten zu werden, denn scheinbar ist kein äußeres Element vorhanden, um die große Last zu stützen. Ein spiralförmiges Element im Inneren der Mauer verleiht dem Tor Stabilität. Ein Sonnendach nimmt die geschwungenen Formen des Eingangs auf. Es hat spiralförmige Zugstange und in das Tor eingelassene Balken, die Bausteine aus Faserzement tragen. Dieses Dach wurde 1965 entfernt und 1977 durch ein kleineres ersetzt.

Rechts neben dem großen Eingang befindet sich ein kleines Eisentor, das als Durchgang für Fußgänger dient. Die Verarbeitung des Metalls ist besonders bemerkenswert, denn dieser so wenig geschmeidige Werkstoff wurde nach seiner Schmalseite hin gebogen. Eine dicke Säule trennt die beiden Eingänge voneinander.

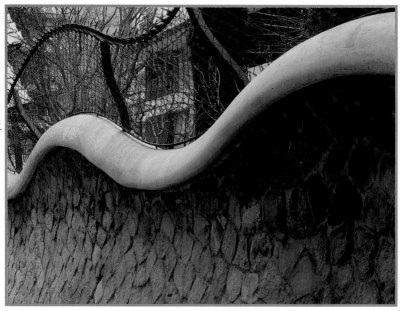

The undulating walls take on a life of their own, like a serpent that guards the estate.

Das helle umlaufende Band unterstreicht zusätzlich die fließende wellenförmige Bewegung der gesamten Mauer.

The roof that crowns the door conceals the boundless imagination demonstrated by the property.

Das Dach, das die Tür krönt, kaschiert die enorme Fantasie, die von dem Grundstück ausgeht.

530

The project is located near the dragon door of the Güell estate. Both projects feature exceptional ironwork, though the forms of the door to the Miralles estate, made up of a system of concentric circles, are more austere.

Diese Arbeit, in der Nähe des Drachentores der Finca Güell, besteht aus wellenförmig ineinander fließenden, von verschiedenen Punkten ausgehenden konzentrischen Kreisen. Auf der Mittelsäule zwischen den beiden Toren sollten die Initialen des Besitzers und das katalanische Wappen in ein großes Medaillon eingelassen werden.

With the help of expert artisans, Gaudí molded iron at will and made this material take on expressive forms full of symbolism.

Bei fachkundigen Handwerkern ließ Gaudí Eisen nach seinen Vorstellungen schmieden und erreichte damit, dass dieser Werkstoff Formen voller intensiver Ausdruckskraft und Symbolik annahm.

Railings, windows, gratings, banisters, doors, balconies and benches… all were susceptible to reinterpretation in wrought iron. Gaudí designed these elements for constructional purposes, but also for ornamentation.

Gitter, Fenster, Zäune, Geländer, Türen, Balkone, Bänke … alles bietet sich dazu an, neu gedeutet und in Schmiedeeisen hergestellt zu werden. Für Gaudí sind es bauliche Elemente, die aber auch einem ornamentalen Anspruch standhalten müssen.

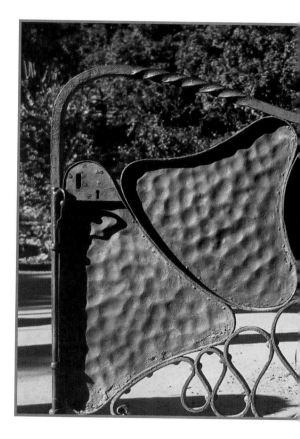

543

Catedral de
Palma de Mallorca

1903-1914

In 1889, when Bishop Pere Campins i Barceló met Gaudí during the construction of the Sagrada Família, he was fascinated by Gaudí's artistic and architectural talent, but mostly by his knowledge of the Catholic liturgy. Years later, the cathedral chapter approved Campins' proposal to restore the cathedral in Palma, one of the most beautiful examples of Catalan gothic architecture, and assigned the project to Gaudí.

The architect's ambitious design aimed to emphasize the building's Gothic character. First, Gaudí relocated certain elements: he moved the choir stalls from the nave to the presbytery and the small choir to a side chapel. He also removed the Baroque altar to discover the old Gothic one. Gaudí also designed new pieces to embellish and amplify the space, including the railings, lights, and liturgical furnishings. He also reinforced the structure, having perceived a slight sagging of the columns.

The relocation of elements made the altar the centerpiece, for which Gaudí designed an octagonal baldachin with symbolic references. The corners allude to the seven virtues of the Holy Spirit and the 50 small lamps refer to the celebration of the Pentecost.

Gaudí's project not only involved the restoration of the building, but also the remodeling of some of the aspects of the liturgy. For the most conservative members of the congregation, Gaudí's intervention deviated too much from the rules, and problems arose as they did in Astorga. Gaudí left the work unfinished to concentrate his efforts on the Sagrada Família.

Im Jahr 1889 lernte Bischof Pere Campins i Barceló Gaudí bei den Arbeiten an der Sagrada Família kennen und war fasziniert von dessen architektonischem und künstlerischem Talent. Vor allem aber beeindruckte ihn Gaudís Kenntnis der katholischen Liturgie. Jahre später billigte das Domkapitel den Vorschlag Campins, die Kathedrale von Palma de Mallorca zu restaurieren, eines der schönsten katalanischen Beispiele gotischer Architektur.

Der ehrgeizige Entwurf sollte den gotischen Charakter des Bauwerkes hervorheben. Das Chorgestühl wurde vom Mittelschiff ins Presbyterium und der kleine Seitenchor in eine Nebenkapelle verlegt. Zudem wurde der Barockaltar entfernt und der alte gotische Altar freigelegt. Außerdem wurden neue Elemente wie Gitter, Leuchter und liturgisches Mobiliar zur Verschönerung und Erweiterung des Raumes hinzugefügt.

Die Umordnung der Ausstattung stellte den Altar in den Vordergrund, für den Gaudí einen siebeneckigen Baldachin mit symbolischen Bezügen entwarf. Die sieben Ecken spielen auf die sieben Gaben des Heiligen Geistes an, und fünfzig kleine Lampen nehmen Bezug auf das Pfingstfest.

Das Vorhaben umfasste nicht nur die Restaurierung des Gebäudes, sondern auch Reformen einiger Elemente der abgehaltenen Liturgie. Da den erzkonservativen Kirchenvertretern der Beitrag Gaudís jedoch zu weit ging, kam es ebenso wie in Astorga zu Problemen mit der Geistlichkeit. Gaudí ließ die Bauarbeiten unvollendet und konzentrierte sich auf die Arbeiten an der Sagrada Família, wo er nicht mit Einschränkungen seines Schaffensdranges rechnen musste.

Due to various reforms, the building had an eclectic style that included influences from Central European architecture and traces of Moorish elements.

Durch mehrere Restaurierungen bekam das Gebäude einen eklektischen Stil, der auf mitteleuropäische Einflüsse und maurische Elemente zurückzuführen ist.

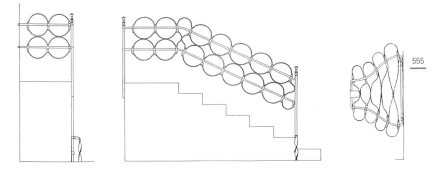

Door and railing of the Corpus Christi gallery
While Gaudí's reorganization of the interior was limited to a certain space, his numerous ironwork designs are found throughout the cathedral, including on the exterior. Of particular interest are the doors and railings formed by united circles and supported by banisters.

Tür und Geländer zur Corpus-Christi-Empore
Die Umstrukturierung des Innenraums sah auch zahlreiche Entwürfe für Schmiedearbeiten sowohl innerhalb als auch außerhalb der Kathedrale vor. Besonders die Türen und Geländer aus aneinandergesetzten, von Rundstäben gehaltenen Ringen wecken das Interesse des Betrachters.

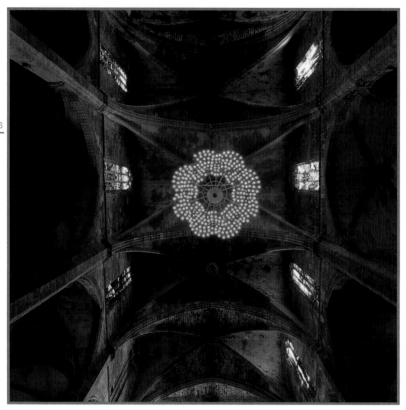

Gaudí's intervention in the cathedral of Palma de Mallorca complied with the ideals of an ecclesiastical reform that found it imperative to adapt the liturgy to the era's evolution of slightly out of date thought.

Gaudís Arbeit an der Kathedrale von Palma de Mallorca orientierte sich an den Idealen einer Kirchenreform, die er für unumgänglich hielt. Diese sollte die überholte Liturgie der geistigen Entwicklung seiner Zeit anpassen.

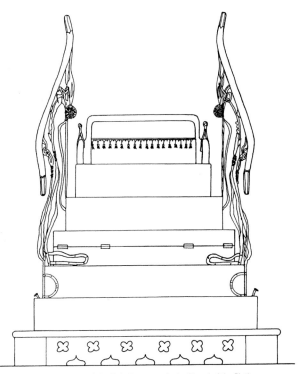

Stairway of the exposition of the Holy Sacrament in the Chapel of the Pietà
Treppe zum Tabernakel in der Kapelle der Pietà

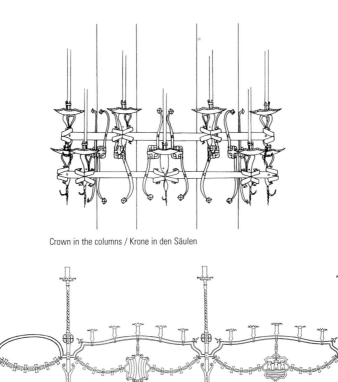

Crown in the columns / Krone in den Säulen

Railing of the presbytery / Geländer des Pfarrhauses

The rings that hold up the columns of the central nave are situated 16 feet above ground and support candles with small trays to catch the wax. The structural system comprises pieces inserted in the stone, and rivets support the candelabras.

In einer Höhe von fünf Metern über dem Boden hängen Kandelaber an sämtlichen Säulen. Unterhalb der Kerzen sind kleine Auffangteller für das herunterfließende Wachs montiert. Die Kandelaber sind mit Bolzen an Eisenbändern befestigt, die in den Stein eingelassen sind.

Gaudí's unmistakable designs are apparent in even the smallest details of the cathedral, such as the delicate wooden benches painted an old-gold color and the ornaments displayed in the confessional.

Die unverwechselbaren Spuren Gaudís sind sogar in den kleinsten Details zu finden, die der Besucher bei seinem Gang durch die Kathedrale entdeckt, so zum Beispiel die zierlichen, mit altgoldener Farbe bemalten Schemel oder die Verzierungen des Beichtstuhls.

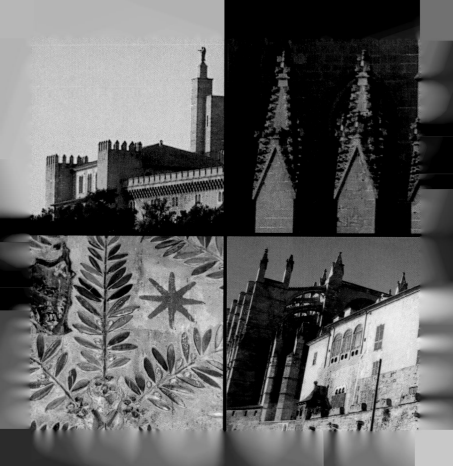

Casa Batlló

1904-1906

The Batlló house, situated on Barcelona's Passeig de Gràcia was constructed in 1877. Its owner, textile manufacturer Josep Batlló i Casanovas, commissioned Gaudí to remodel the façade and redistribute the courtyards. Marked by Gaudí's personal touch, the Batlló house became one of the most emblematic projects of his extensive career.

The exterior of the building is covered with stones from Marés and glass on the first floors, while ceramic disks shroud the upper floors. During the renovation, the architect stood on the street and decided the position of each piece so that it would stand out and shine with impact. This manner of working, namely improving and perfecting an initial idea during the construction process, recurs in all of Gaudí's works and reflects his dedication to his projects. Since the authorities had to approve only finished projects, this method caused some bureaucratic problems. To avoid these conflicts, Gaudí sketched the plans of his projects, allowing for their evolution during construction.

The poetry of the façade culminates in the roof of the attic, which is topped with pinkish-blue ceramic pieces in the form of scales and a base of spherical and cylindrical pieces that evokes the back of a dragon. A cylindrical tower crowned by a small convex cross finishes off the building, which, despite its surprising colors and innovative geometry, blends with its location and the height of the neighboring buildings.

On the roof, the chimneys and water cisterns were covered with pieces of glass and colored ceramic pieces, fixed on top of a mortar base.

Die Casa Batlló, am Passeig de Gràcia in Barcelona gelegen, existiert seit 1877. Sein Besitzer, der Textilfabrikant Josep Batlló i Casanovas beauftragte Gaudí damit, die Fassade neu zu gestalten und die Lichthöfe neu anzuordnen. Gaudí gab dem Projekt eine sehr persönliche Note, und das Haus wurde zu einem der emblematischsten Werke seiner Laufbahn.

Die Fassade wurde im unteren Teil mit Marés-Stein und Glas und im oberen Teil mit Keramik verkleidet. Während der Bauarbeiten legte Gaudí selbst die Position der einzelnen Teile fest, damit sie auffielen und glänzten. Diese Vorgehensweise, während des Bauprozesses Verbesserungen vorzunehmen, ist typisch für seine Arbeit. Das brachte ihm Schwierigkeiten ein, da die Behörden nur abgeschlossene Projekte genehmigen durften. Um einen Konflikt zu vermeiden, fertigte Gaudí Entwürfe zur Genehmigung an und entwickelte sie im Verlauf der Arbeiten fort.

Die Poesie der Fassade findet ihren Höhepunkt im Dach. Es ist mit rosa-bläulichen schuppenförmigen Keramikziegeln und einem First aus runden und zylindrischen Teilen bedeckt. Es erinnert an den Körper eines Drachens und wird von einem Turm mit bauchigem Kreuz gekrönt. Trotz der überraschenden Geometrie und Farben berücksichtigte Gaudí die Lage des Hauses und passte es der Höhe der Nachbargebäude an. Das Dach, die Schornsteine und die Wasserreservoirs sind mit bunter Keramik und Glasstücken verkleidet.

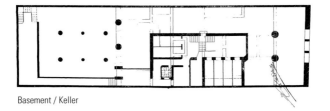

Basement / Keller

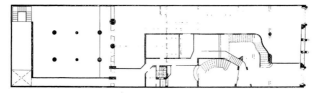

Ground floor / Erdgeschoss

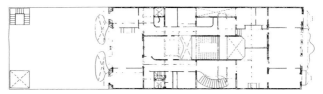

First floor / Erstes Obergeschoss

The polychromy of the stone, the ceramic pieces, and the stained glass windows are a metaphor of a rural vision: under the purple of the mountains are all the luminous shades of morning dew.

Die Vielfarbigkeit des Steins, die Keramiksteinchen und die Fenster: All das sind Metaphern für den Zauber eines Sonnenaufgangs auf dem Lande. In den dunkel-violetten Tönen sind alle funkelnden Nuancen des Morgentaus enthalten.

The courtyard around which the staircase winds is covered with ceramic pieces. High up, they are ultramarine blue, and their color slowly softens until it becomes white on the ground floor. This chromatic gradation causes a uniform reflection of the light, creating similar tones throughout the height of the patio. From the caretaker's quarters, one sees a uniform pearl-gray.

Die Eingangshalle um die Treppe herum ist mit Keramiksteinchen bedeckt. Diese sind oben zunächst ultramarinblau und werden nach und nach immer heller, bis sie unten am Boden ganz weiß sind. Durch die chromatische Reduzierung wird das Licht auf einzigartige Weise zurückgeworfen und bringt ähnliche Reflexe auf der ganzen Höhe des Eingangsbereiches hervor.

Throughout the building, one can appreciate the architect's desire to create continuous spaces, since there are no arrises, corners or right angles. Partitions exist because of curvaceous transitions that evoke organic forms.

Im gesamten Gebäude spiegelt sich der Wunsch des Architekten wider, endlose Räume zu schaffen, ohne Ecken, Kanten oder rechte Winkel. Kurvenreiche Übergänge schaffen eine Aufteilung, die an organische Formen erinnert.

The chimney of the hall is one of the practical devices used by Gaudí to endow the spaces with quality and comfort.

Der Kamin im Foyer ist einer der praktischen Einfälle, durch die Gaudí den Räumen Wärme und Behaglichkeit verlieh.

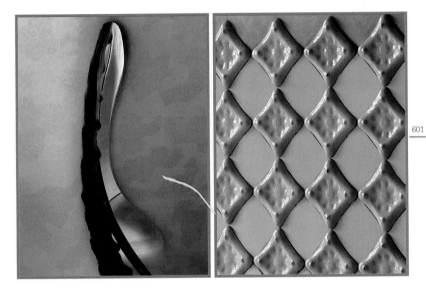

The artist's boundless imagination is evident in the details of the screen that divides the room of the oratory, and in the door of the hall. The works of marquetry commissioned by Gaudí were created in the workshops of Casas y Bardés. The oratory, which is still owned by the Batlló family, includes diverse pieces, like the Sagrada Família by Josep Llimona.

Die grenzenlose Vorstellungskraft des Künstlers macht sich in den Details auf der Trennwand des Oratoriums bemerkbar. Die von Gaudí in Auftrag gegebenen Einlegearbeiten wurden in der Werkstatt von Casas y Bardés hergestellt. Das Oratorium, das noch heute der Batlló-Familie gehört, besteht aus unterschiedlichen Stücken, wie die Sagrada Família des Josep Llimona.

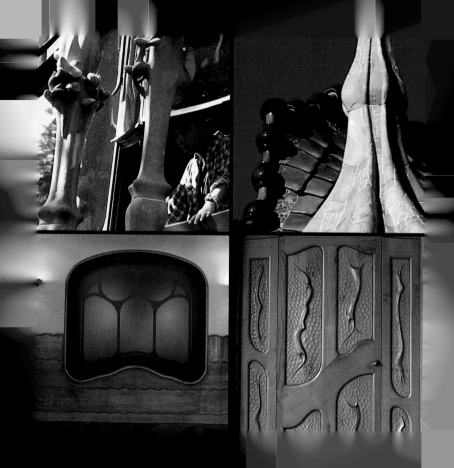

608

Gaudí was convinced that nature was the medium by which the earth became the friend and master of man. Nature inspired the designs of Gaudí.

Gaudí war davon überzeugt, dass die Natur die Erde zur Freundin und Meisterin des Menschen machen könne. Viele seiner Entwürfe sind daher von der Natur inspiriert.

Expressionist naturalism runs throughout his work. His constructions often appear as living organisms. Gaudí's sensibility and genius allowed him to live in a world created by his own fantasies.

Der expressionistische Naturalismus zieht sich durch Gaudís gesamtes Werk. Seine Konstruktionen wirken oft wie lebendige Organismen, und durch seine feinfühlige und geniale Art schuf er eine ganz eigene Fantasiewelt.

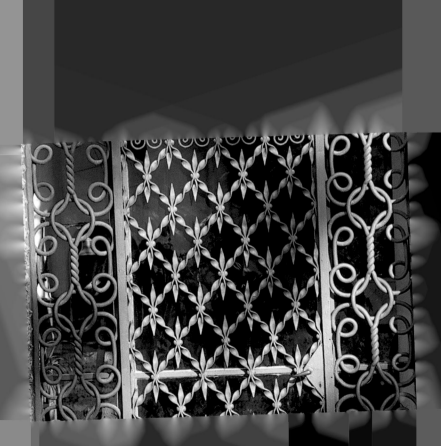

Gaudí chose to liberate forms from the restricted and cold academics that prevailed during his era. Common elements, like doors, are presented with expressivity and imagination, and are free of formal limitations.

Gaudí befreite einige der alltäglichen Elemente, wie beispielsweise Türen, vom Korsett des kalten akademischen Stils seiner Zeit und weitete ihre formalen Grenzen aus, indem er sie ausdrucksstark und fantasievoll gestaltete.

During Gaudí's time, it was possible to develop any form, idea or color. This permitted him to fill his works with revolutionary concepts. Creative art formed part of the architect's buildings and was an expression of his personality.

Gaudí bereicherte seine Bauwerke mit schöpferischen, oft revolutionären Konzepten von Formen, Ideen und Farben. Diese sind Bestandteil der Gebäude und Ausdruck der Persönlichkeit des Architekten.

Casa Milà, located on the corner of Passeig de Gràcia and Carrer Provença, rises up like a large, rocky formation and ever since its construction, Barceloneses have called it La Pedrera ("The Stone Quarry"). Commissioned by Pere Milà and his wife Roser Segimon, Gaudí took the opportunity to make up for the lack of monuments in Barcelona, about which he often complained.

Because of the building's large dimensions, Gaudí limited the number of materials. He substituted load-bearing walls for a system of main beams and pillars, and carefully designed the links in order to reduce their section. He also envisioned a seemingly heavy and forceful façade, which, in reality, is formed by slim limestone plaques from Garraf on the lower part and from Vilafranca on the upper levels. The amount of iron used would make any sculptural expert tremble. The sinuous forms of the façade are reflected inside, where right angles and fixed partition walls are nonexistent, and every detail is drawn to the millimeter.

Gaudí let his imagination run wild on the roof, where the staircase boxes are extravagant volumes covered with small ceramic pieces. The helical forms of the chimneys emphasize the whirl of the smoke. Even though Gaudí never finished the project because of a disagreement with the client, Casa Milà is one of the most complete examples of Gaudí architecture. The house displays intelligent constructional solutions, a striking compositional sensibility and an exuberant imagination.

Die Casa Milà, ein Auftrag von Pere Milà und seiner Frau Roser Segimón, steht an der Ecke Passeig de Gràcia / Carrer Provença. Sie sieht aus wie eine Felsformation, weshalb die Einwohner Barcelonas sie auch La Pedrera (Steinbruch) nennen. Gaudí bemängelte das Fehlen monumentaler Bauwerke in Barcelona und wollte damit Abhilfe schaffen.

Das Gebäude hat gewaltige Ausmaße, sodass sich Gaudí eine Möglichkeit zur Materialeinsparung ausdenken musste. Zunächst ersetzte er tragende Wände durch ein System von Balken und Säulen, auf deren Verbindungen er sein Augenmerk richtete, um ihren Querschnitt zu verringern. Außerdem arbeitete er mit einer scheinbar soliden Fassade aus Stein, die aber nur aus dünnen Kalksteinplatten bestand, die für den unteren Teil aus dem Garraf und für den oberen aus Vilafranca kamen. Die Menge der benutzten Eisenträger ließ manchen Experten zittern. Die Formen der Fassade finden ihre Entsprechung im Inneren. Dort gibt es keinen rechten Winkel, es existieren keine unverrückbaren Zwischenwände, und sämtliche Details sind millimetergenau gezeichnet.

Gaudí ließ seiner Fantasie auch auf dem Dach freien Lauf: Ebenso wie die Treppenhäuser, die zu extravaganten Räumen werden, sind auch die Schornsteine mit Mosaiken verkleidet, deren Spiralform die wirbelnde Bewegung des Rauchs nachempfindet. Unstimmigkeiten mit den Kunden führten dazu, dass der Architekt das Projekt unvollendet ließ. Dennoch ist die Casa Milà eines der am vollständigsten erhaltenen Gebäude Gaudís.

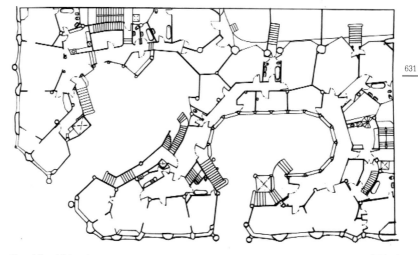

Ground floor / Erdgeschoss

0 2 4

"It would not surprise me if, in the future, this house became a hotel, given the easy way to change the distributions, and the abundance of bathrooms."

„Es würde mich nicht wundern, wenn dieses Haus eines Tages als großes Hotel genutzt würde – schon deshalb, weil man die Grundrisse leicht verändern kann und es viele Badezimmer gibt."

The chimneys on the terrace roof look like mythical creatures and rise up above the façade of Casa Milà, so that pedestrians can admire them from the Passeig de Gràcia. Some of the chimneys are covered with small colored ceramic pieces (*trencadís*) and others with glass chips from champagne bottles.

Die wie Fabeltiere oder Figuren gestalteten Schornsteine ragen über die Fassade der Casa Milà hinaus, sodass sie die Fußgänger auf dem Passeig de Gràcia von der Straße aus bewundern können. Einige wurden mit kleinen farbigen Keramikscherben, andere mit Glasscherben von Champagnerflaschen verziert.

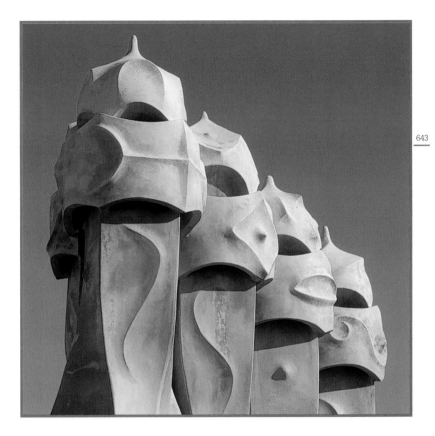

"Vegetation is the means by which the earth becomes man's companion, his friend, his teacher."

„Die Vegetation ist das Medium, das die Erde zur Gefährtin des Menschen werden lässt, zu seiner Freundin und Lehrmeisterin."

As with the façade, all the constructional elements of the interior have a sculptural character. A good example of this is the false ceilings which have no right angles. The forms that adorn the plaster finishes evoke the foam of waves and reproduce floral motifs and inscriptions, most of them religious.

Wie bei der Fassade wirken auch sämtliche Bauelemente im Inneren wie Skulpturen. Beispiele hierfür sind die Zwischendecken, die niemals rechte Winkel aufweisen. Die Stuckarbeiten erinnern an die bewegte Oberfläche des Meeres, empfinden florale Motive nach oder zeigen religiöse Inschriften.

The chimneys are disguised by sculptural pieces that represent the image of medieval warriors. They are crowned with forms inspired by nature or covered with *trencadís* to break the chromatic monotony.

Wie rätselhafte Wesen aus einer anderen Welt wirken die Formen der Schornsteine und Belüftungsrohre, von denen es auf den Dachterrassen der Pedrera oder des Palau Güell nur so wimmelt.

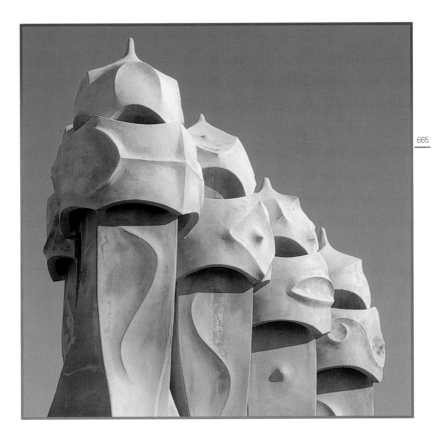

The diverse figures that cover the terrace roofs of buildings like the Pedrera or Palau Güell are enigmatic chimneys or ventilation tubes that once again demonstrate Gaudí's creative talent.

Die verschiedenen Figuren auf den Dachterrassen der Pedrera oder des Palau Güell sind schillernde Schornsteine oder Belüftungsrohre. Auch sie spiegeln Gaudís kreatives Talent wider.

Jardins Artigas

1905

After an extensive study conducted by the Gaudí Real Cátedra, it was determined that Gaudí had in fact designed the gardens surrounding the old Artigas factory, in the province of Barcelona. The architect received the assignment when he visited the prosperous industrialist, Joan Artigas i Alart, at his home in La Pobla de Lillet.

The estate is located on the banks where the River Llobregat rises, which presented the architect with the opportunity to design the only "moist garden" of his career. The site is elongated and follows the course of the river. A bridge marks the natural entrance to the property and leads the visitor to a cave and a spectacular natural fountain called La Magnèsia, the name by which the project is widely known.

A winding path leads to the second bridge where Gaudí intervened by building a small cylindrical arbor surrounded by dry-stone walls and covered with a pointed dome. Further along the path, the visitor reaches the last bridge that Gaudí designed, which features stones that hang like stalactites. One extreme transforms into a pergola that shelters visitors from inclement weather.

Apart from tracing and embellishing the site's path along the river, Gaudí also added numerous flowerbeds and indigenous bushes, put up small walls covered by ceramic pieces and distributed various sculptures around the park.

The similarities between the Artigas Gardens and Park Güell are many: the symbolism of the sculptures, the use of stone and wood, and certain plants, brought from Park Güell.

Eine ausführliche Studie des Königlichen Gaudí-Lehrstuhls stellte fest, dass die Gärten, welche die alte Artigas-Fabrik in der Provinz Lleida umgeben, von Gaudí entworfen wurden. Der Architekt hatte den Auftrag erhalten, als er den wohlhabenden Industriellen Joan Artigas i Alart in seinem Haus in La Pobla de l'Illet besuchte.

Das Gut liegt an der Quelle des Flusses Llobregat, was dem Architekten die Gelegenheit gab, einen Feuchtgarten anzulegen, den einzigen in seinem Werk. Das Grundstück ist lang gezogen und folgt in seiner Ausdehnung dem Flussverlauf. Eine Brücke markiert den natürlichen Eingang zum Komplex und führt den Besucher zu einer Grotte und zu einer eindrucksvollen natürlichen Quelle. Sie heißt La Magnèsia und gab dem Projekt den Namen, unter dem es bekannt ist.

Ein Weg schlängelt sich zur zweiten Brücke, wo Gaudí eine kleine runde Laube aus Trockensteinmauerwerk, die von einer spitz zulaufenden Kuppel überdacht ist, entwarf. Folgt man dem Weg, gelangt man zur letzten Brücke, von der Steine wie Stalaktiten herabhängen. Ein Ende der Brücke wird zur Pergola, die Besuchern bei schlechtem Wetter Schutz bietet.

Gaudí entwarf auch zahlreiche Rabatten mit einheimischen Blumen und Büschen, errichtete kleine mit Keramik verkleidete Mauern und verteilte mehrere Skulpturen über den ganzen Park.

Die Ähnlichkeit zum Park Güell sind unverkennbar. Sie zeigt sich in der Symbolik der Skulpturen, der Verwendung von Stein und Holz, sowie in den Pflanzen, die vom Park Güell herangeschafft wurden.

Even though Gaudí used similar resources to those of Park Güell, here he included an element absent in other projects: water, which he used to create a fantastic, moist garden.

Obwohl Gaudí ähnliche Mittel wie im Park Güell verwendete, verfügte er hier über ein zusätzliches Element: Wasser. Er setzte es so geschickt ein, dass hier ein fantastischer Feuchtgarten entstand.

The garden path follows the upper reaches of the River Llobregat.

Die Anlage des Gartens begleitet den Fluss Llobregat, der hier entspringt, in seinem ersten Abschnitt.

Even though the symbolism is repeated in most of the architect's projects, the figures of this work do not represent any story. They are only figures of animals and characters, and have nothing to do with mythology or religion.

Obwohl sich der Symbolismus in vielen Werken Gaudís wiederfindet, sind diese Figuren lediglich Tiere, die keine tiefere religiöse oder mythologische Bedeutung haben.

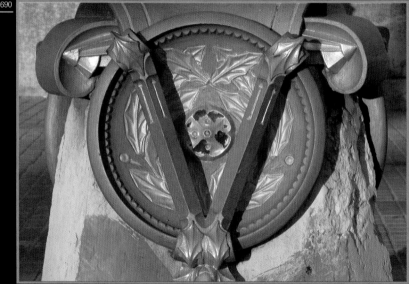

Casa Vicens

Carolines, 24-26, Barcelona

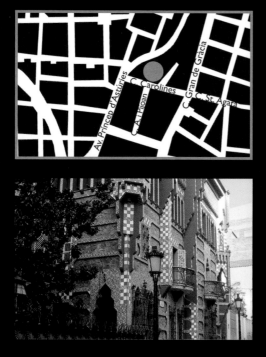

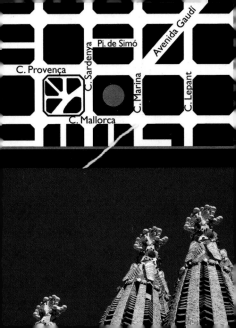

C. Provença

C. Sardenya

Pj. de Simó

Avenida Gaudí

C. Marina

C. Lepant

C. Mallorca

C. Mérida

C. Alcolea

C. Panero

Palacio Episcopal
de Astorga

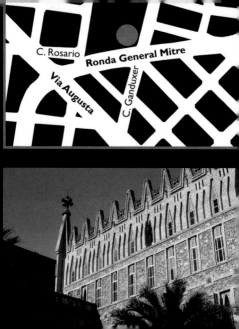

C. Rosario

Ronda General Mitre

Via Augusta

C. Ganduxer

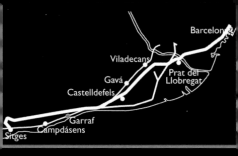

Barcelon[a]

Viladecans

Gavá

Prat del
Llobregat

Castelldefels

Garraf

Campdásens

Sitges

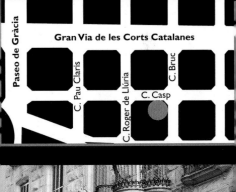

Paseo de Gràcia

Gran Via de les Corts Catalanes

C. Pau Claris

C. Roger de Llúria

C. Casp

C. Bruc

Cripta de la Colònia Güell

Reixac, s/n, Sta. Coloma de Cervelló, Barcelona

Bellesguard

Bellesguard, 16-20, Barcelona

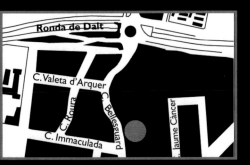

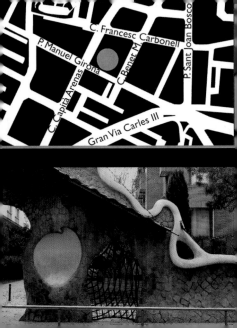

C. Palau Reial

Antoni Maura

Seu

General

Plaza
Almoina

C. Dalt Murada

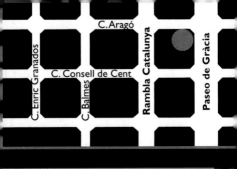

C. Aragó

C. Enric Granados

C. Consell de Cent

C. Balmes

Rambla Catalunya

Paseo de Gràcia

Jardins Artigas

La Pobla de Lillet, Barcelona

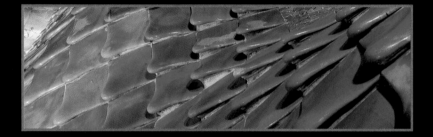

Unconstructed projects

Nicht realisierte Entwürfe

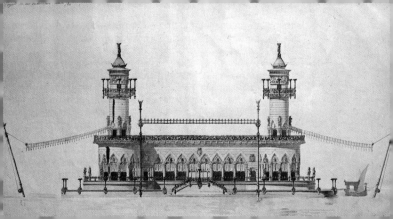

Unconstructed projects

Nicht realisierte Entwürfe

When the crypt of the Sagrada Família was burned in 1936, much of the graphic documentation that the architect kept with him disappeared. However, Gaudí was not an architect who relied solely on plans; he also worked with models and preferred to make changes during the construction, as the project developed. The lack of information has led to many speculations about his creations. Almost a century later, we are still discovering new work by the brilliant architect. This book presents only some of the projects that he designed but never constructed. We feature some of the most important ones in this chapter.

Mit dem Brand in der Krypta der Sagrada Família im Jahr 1936 ging umfassendes grafisches Dokumentationsmaterial verloren. Zudem war Gaudí nie ein Freund von Zeichnungen gewesen, da er viel mit Modellen arbeitete und ohnehin im Zuge der fortschreitenden Arbeiten häufig Änderungen an den Bauwerken vornahm. Dieser Mangel an Information gab zu zahlreichen Spekulationen über sein Schaffen Anlass, und auch nach fast einem Jahrhundert werden immer wieder neue Beweise für die Tätigkeit des genialen Architekten entdeckt. Da nur wenige Unterlagen zu seinen nicht verwirklichten Projekten vorhanden sind, werden in diesem Kapitel lediglich einige der bedeutendsten vorgestellt.

In 1882, Gaudí designed a hunting pavilion for Eusebi Güell on an extensive property that Güell owned on the coasts of Garraf, to the south of Barcelona. The pavilion was never constructed. Instead, Gaudí built Bodegas Güell on the land, with the collaboration of Francesc Berenguer. The pavilion is reminiscent of the Casa Vicens and El Capricho.

1882 entwarf Gaudí einen Jagdpavillon für Güell auf einem ausgedehnten Gut südlich von Barcelona. Er wurde nie gebaut, aber auf dem Gelände errichtete der Architekt in Zusammenarbeit mit Francesc Berenguer die Bodegas Güell. Der Pavillon erinnert an die Casa Vicens und an El Capricho, beides Werke, an denen er in jener Zeit arbeitete.

In 1876, when Gaudí was still studying, he designed the colonnade of a covered patio for the Council of Barcelona. The capitals and the arches are decorated with floral motifs that Gaudí repeated in many of his works.

1876, während Gaudí noch an der Hochschule für Architektur in Barcelona studierte, entwarf er die Kolonnade eines überdachten Innenhofes für die Provinzialverwaltung von Barcelona. Kapitelle und Bögen waren mit floralen Motiven verziert, die sich im Laufe seines Schaffens immer wiederholen sollten.

The Marquis of Comillas
commissioned Gaudí to design a
building for Franciscan missionaries
in the Moroccan city of Tangier.
After a trip to the site in 1892,
Gaudí began to draw the project,
which he finished the following
year.

Im Auftrag des Grafen von Comillas
entwarf Gaudí ein Gebäude für die
Franziskaner-Missionare in der
marokkanischen Stadt Tanger. Nach
einer Reise zu den Mönchen im
Jahre 1892 begann er mit den
Entwürfen für das Projekt, die er im
darauffolgenden Jahr beendete.

In 1908, an American businessman, seduced by Gaudí's talent, commissioned him to design a large hotel in Manhattan. The architect envisioned an ambitious, 987-foot high building that recalled the Sagrada Família. Only a few original drawings remain of the hotel.

1908 entwarf Gaudí für einen nordamerikanischen Unternehmer ein großes Hotel in Manhattan: ein ehrgeiziges Projekt von 300 Metern Höhe, das an die Sagrada Família erinnerte und von dem nur noch wenige Zeichnungen erhalten sind.

Though Gaudí did not win the special prize that he longed for with this project, he did demonstrate that, even as a student, his skill and imagination had no limits. The drawing's details and formal complexity reveal the young architect's talent.

Auch wenn Gaudí nie den mit diesem Projekt angestrebten Sonderpreis erhielt, so bewies er doch bereits während seiner Zeit als Student, dass sein Fachwissen und sein Einfallsreichtum keine Grenzen kannten. Die Detailgenauigkeit und die formale Komplexität der Zeichnungen lassen das enorme Talent des Genies erahnen.

Gaudí by night

Gaudí bei Nacht

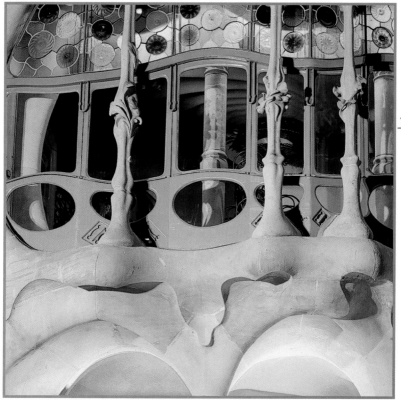

Chronology and bibliography

Chronologie und Bibliografie

Chronology of the life and work of Antoni Gaudí

1852 Born in Reus, Tarragona; son of Francesc Gaudí i Serra and Antònia Cornet y Bertran.

1867 First drawings in the magazine "El Arlequín" of Reus, Tarragona.

1867-1870 Collaborated with Josep Ribera and Eduard Toda on the restoration of the Poblet monastery.

1873-1878 Studies at the Escuela Técnica Superior d´Arquitectura de Barcelona.

1876 Design for the Spanish Pavilion at the Centennial International Exhibition in Philadelphia. School projects: patio of a Provincial Delegation and a jetty. Death of his mother.

1877 Design of a monumental fountain for Plaça de Catalunya, Barcelona. Plans for the Hospital General in Barcelona. Designed an auditorium as the final project for his degree.

1878 Design of the streetlamps for Plaça Reial (inaugurated in September, 1879). Draft of Casa Vicens. Store window for the glove shop of Esteve Comella, which captured the attention of Eusebi Güell, who became his patron.

1882 Collaborated with Josep Fontserè on the Parc de la Ciutadella. Gaudí personally designed the entrance doors and the cascade.

1878-1882 Design of the Textile Worker's Cooperative of Mataró. Plan for a kiosk for Enrique Girosi.

1879 Decoration of the Gibert pharmacy on Passeig de Gràcia in Barcelona (demolished in 1895). Death of his sister Rosita Gaudí de Egea.

1880 Plan for the electric illumination of the seawall in collaboration with Josep Serramalera.

1882 Design of a hunting pavilion commissioned by Eusebi Güell on the coast of Garraf, Barcelona.

1883 Drawing of the altar for the Santo Sacramento chapel for the parish church of Alella, Barcelona.

1883-1888 House for Manuel Vicens on Carrer Carolines in Barcelona. In 1925, the architect Joan Baptista Serra Martínez enlarged the space between two supporting walls, modifying the walls and the property limits.

1883-1885 House for Don Máximo Díaz de Quijano, widely known as El Capricho (The Caprice), in Comillas, Santander. The head of construction was Cristóbal Cascante, architect and school companion of Gaudí.

1884-1887 Pavilions of the Finca Güell: caretaker's quarters and stables on Avenida Pedralbes in Barcelona. The pavilions now house the headquarters of the Real Cátedra Gaudí, inaugurated in 1953, belonging to the Escuela Técnica Superior de Arquitectura de Barcelona.

1883-1926 Temple Expiatori de la Sagrada Família.

1886-1888 Palau Güell, residence of Eusebi Güell and his family on the Nou de La Rambla in Barcelona. Since 1954, the building has housed the headquarters of Barcelona's Museum of Theatre.

1887 Drawing of the Pavilion of the Transatlantic Company at the Naval Exhibition in Cádiz.

1888-1889 Palacio episcopal de Astorga, León. Gaudí received the commission from the bishop of Astorga, Joan Baptista Grau i Vallespinós. In 1893, following the bishop's death, he abandoned the project, which Ricard Guereta later finished.

1889-1893 Colegio de las Teresianas on the Ganduxer in Barcelona, commissioned by Enrique d'Ossó, founder of the order.

1892-1893 The home of Fernández Andrés, widely known as Casa de los Botines in León.

1895 Bodegas Güell on the coast of Garraf, Barcelona, in collaboration with Francesc Berenguer.

1898-1900 Casa Calvet, on the Casp in Barcelona.

1900-1909 Home of Jaume Figueres, known as Bellesguard. Joan Rubió i Bellver helped manage the project.

1900-1914 Park Güell, on Barcelona's "Bald Mountain," commissioned by Eusebi Güell and with the collaboration of Josep Maria Jujol. In 1922, it became municipal property.

1901-1902 Door and wall of the estate of Hermenegild Miralles on Passeig Manuel Girona in Barcelona.

1902 Renovation of the house of the Marqués of Castelldosrius, on the Nova Junta de Comerç in Barcelona.
Decoration of Café Torino, commissioned by Ricard Company and with the collaboration of Pere Falqués, Lluís Domènech i Montaner and Josep Puig i Cadafalch. The café, which no longer exists, was located on Passeig de Gràcia in Barcelona.

1903-1914 Remodeling of the cathedral in Palma de Mallorca, commissioned by Pere Campins and with the collaboration of Francesc Berenguer, Joan Rubió i Bellver and Josep Maria Jujol.

1904 House project for Lluís Graner.

1904-1906 Remodeling of Casa Batlló on Passeig de Gràcia in Barcelona, commissioned by Josep Batlló i Casanovas and with the collaboration of Josep Maria Jujol.

1906 Death of his father.

1906-1910 Casa Milà, widely known as La Pedrera on Passeig de Gràcia in Barcelona, commissioned by Rosario Segimon de Milà and with the collaboration of Josep Maria Jujol.

1908-1916 Crypt of the Colònia Güell in Santa Coloma de Cervelló, Barcelona. Construction began in 1908 and was supervised by Francesc Berenguer. The act of consecration took place November 3, 1915.

1908 Gaudí was commissioned to construct a hotel in New York, which remained only a sketch.

1909-1910 School of the Temple Expiatori de la Sagrada Família.

1910 The work of Gaudí is displayed at the Société Nationale de Beaux-Arts in Paris.

1912 Pulpits for the parish church of Blanes, Girona. Death of his niece Rosa Egea i Gaudí at the age of 36.

1914 Death of his friend and collaborator Francesc Berenguer. Decides to work exclusively on the Sagrada Família.

1923 Studies for the chapel of the Colònia Calvet in Torelló, Barcelona.

1924 Pulpit for a church in Valencia.

1926 Gaudí is hit by a tram on June 7 and dies three days later at the Hospital de la Santa Creu in Barcelona.

Chronologie des Lebens und der Werke Antoni Gaudís

1852 Geburt in Reus, Tarragona; Sohn von Francesc Gaudí i Serra und Antònia Cornet i Bertran.

1867 Erste Zeichnungen in der Zeitschrift „El Arlequín" in Reus, Tarragona.

1867–1870 Zusammenarbeit mit Josep Ribera und Eduard Toda am Projekt der Restaurierung des Klosters Poblet.

1873–1878 Studium an der Hochschule für Architektur in Barcelona.

1876 Entwurf für den spanischen Ausstellungspavillon zur Hundertjahrfeier Philadelphias; Entwürfe im Rahmen des Studiums: Innenhof der Provinzialverwaltung sowie eine Bootsanlegestelle; Tod der Mutter.

1877 Entwurf eines monumentalen Springbrunnens für die Plaça de Catalunya, Barcelona. Entwurf für das Krankenhaus Hospital General in Barcelona. Entwurf einer Aula als Studienabschlussprojekt.

1878 Entwurf der Laternen der Plaça Real (eingeweiht im September 1879). Vorprojekt für die Casa Vicens. Schaufenster für den Handschuhmacher Esteban Comella. Das Schaufenster erregt die Aufmerksamkeit von Eusebi Güell, der sein Mäzen wird.

1882 Zusammenarbeit mit Josep Fontserè im Parc de la Ciutadella. Die Eingangstore und die Kaskade sind fast vollständig von Gaudí entworfene Projekte.

1878–1882 Entwurf für die Textilarbeitergenossenschaft von Mataró. Entwurf eines Kiosks für Enrique Girosi.

1879 Dekoration der Apotheke Gibert am Passeig de Gràcia in Barcelona (1895 abgerissen); Tod seiner Schwester Rosita Gaudí de Egea.

1880 Entwurf für die elektrische Beleuchtung der Seepromenade in Zusammenarbeit mit Josep Serramalera.

1882 Entwurf für einen Jagdpavillon im Auftrag Eusebi Güells an der Küste des Garraf, Barcelona.

1883 Zeichnung des Altars für die Kapelle des Heiligen Sakraments der Gemeindekirche von Alella, Barcelona.

1883–1888 Haus für den Kachelfabrikanten Don Manuel Vicens in der Carrer Carolines in Barcelona. 1925 erweitert der Architekt Joan Baptista Serra Martínez die Anlage; Wände und Umfassungsmauer werden verändert.

1883–1885 Haus für Don Máximo Díaz de Quijano, landläufig El Capricho genannt, in Comillas, Santander. Die Leitung der Arbeiten unterliegt Cristóbal Cascante, Architekt und Kommilitone Gaudís.

1884–1887 Pavillons der Finca Güell: Pförtnerhaus und Stallungen in der Avinguda Pedralbes de Barcelona, derzeit Sitz des Königlichen Gaudí-Lehrstuhls, Hochschule für Architektur in Barcelona, eröffnet 1953.

1883–1926 Sagrada Família.

1886–1888 Palau Güell, Wohnhaus für Eusebi Güell und seine Familie in der Carrer Nou de La Rambla in Barcelona, seit 1954 Sitz des Theatermuseums.

1887 Zeichnung des Pavillons der Transatlantikgesellschaft für die Seefahrtsausstellung in Cádiz.

1888–1889 Bischofspalast von Astorga, León. Gaudí erhält den Auftrag aus den Händen des Bischofs von Astorga, Don Joan Baptista Grau i Vallespinós. 1893 gibt er nach dem Tod des Bischofs die Arbeiten auf, die von Guereta zu Ende geführt werden.

1889–1893 Colegio de las Teresianas in der Carrer Ganduxer in Barcelona im Auftrag von Enrique d'Ossó, dem Gründer des Ordens;
Casa Fernández Andrés, landläufig Casa de los Botines genannt, in León.

1895 Bodegas Güell an der Küste des Garraf, Barcelona, in Zusammenarbeit mit Francesc Berenguer.

1898–1900 Casa Calvet, in der Carrer Casp in Barcelona.

1900–1909 Casa de Jaume Figueres, landläufig Bellesguard genannt. In der Bauleitung arbeitet er mit Joan Rubió i Bellver zusammen.

1900–1914 Park Güell auf dem Hügel Muntanya Pelada in Barcelona im Auftrag von Eusebi Güell. Zusammenarbeit mit Josep Maria Jujol. Geht 1922 in Gemeindebesitz über.

1901–1902 Tor und Umfassungsmauer des Grundstücks von Hermenegild Miralles am Passeig Manuel Girona in Barcelona.

1902 Renovierung des Wohnhauses des Markgrafen von Castelldosrius in der Carrer Nova Junta de Comerç in Barcelona. Dekoration des Café Torino im Auftrag von Ricard Company. Das Café, das heute nicht mehr existiert, befand sich am Passeig de Gràcia in Barcelona. An dem Projekt arbeiteten Pere Falqués, Lluís Domènech i Montaner und Josep Puig i Cadafalch mit.

1903–1914 Restaurierung der Kathedrale von Palma de Mallorca im Auftrag des Bischofs Pere Campins mit Francesc Berenguer, Joan Rubió i Bellver und Josep Maria Jujol.

1904   Projekt eines Hauses für Lluís Graner.

1904–1906   Renovierung der Casa Batlló am Passeig de Gràcia in Barcelona im Auftrag von Josep Batlló i Casanovas unter Mitarbeit von Josep Maria Jujol.

1906   Tod des Vaters.

1906–1910   Casa Milà, landläufig La Pedrera genannt, am Passeig de Gràcia in Barcelona, im Auftrag von Rosario Segimon de Milà in Zusammenarbeit mit Josep Maria Jujol.

1908–1916   Krypta der Colònia Güell in Santa Coloma de Cervelló, Barcelona. Die Bauarbeiten begannen 1908 und wurden von Francesc Berenguer überwacht. Die Einweihung fand am 3. November 1915 statt.

1908   Entwürfe für ein Hotel in New York City.

1909–1910   Schulen der Sagrada Família.

1910   Das Werk Gaudís wird in der Société Nationale des Beaux-Arts in Paris ausgestellt.

1912   Kanzeln für die Gemeindekirche in Blanes, Girona; Tod der Nichte Rosa Egea i Gaudí im Alter von 36 Jahren.

1914   Tod seines Freundes und Mitarbeiters Francesc Berenguer. Gaudí entscheidet sich, ausschließlich an der Sagrada Família zu arbeiten.

1923   Studien für die Kapelle der Colònia Calvet in Torelló, Barcelona.

1924   Kanzel für eine Kirche in Valencia.

1926   Gaudí wird am 7. Juni von einer Straßenbahn angefahren und stirbt drei Tage später im Krankenhaus Hospital de la Santa Creu in Barcelona.

Bibliography

Bibliografie

754

Bassegoda i Nonell, Joan I., *Gaudí. Arquitectura del futur*. Barcelona, Editorial Salvat para la Caixa de Pensions, 1984.

Castellar-Gassol, Joan, *Gaudí. La vida de un visionario*. Barcelona, Edicions 1984, 1999.

Collins, George R., *Antonio Gaudí*. 1962.

Garcia, Raül, *Barcelona y Gaudí. Ejemplos modernistas*. Barcelona, H. Kliczkowski, 2000.

Garcia, Raül, *Gaudí y el Modernismo en Barcelona*. Barcelona, H. Kliczkowski, 2001.

Güell, Xavier, *Antoni Gaudí*. Barcelona, Ed. Gustavo Gili, 1987.

Lahuerta, J. J. , *Gaudí i el seu temps*. Barcelona, Barcanova, 1990.

Llarch, J. , *Gaudí, biografía mágica*. Barcelona, Plaza & Janés, 1982.

Martinell, Cèsar, *Gaudí. Su vida, su teoría, su obra*. Barcelona, Col·legi d'Arquitectes de Catalunya, 1967.

Martinell, Cèsar, *Gaudí i la Sagrada Família comentada per ell mateix*. Barcelona, Editorial Aymà, 1941.

Morrione, G. *Gaudí. Immagine e architettura*. Roma, Kappa ed., 1979.

Ràfols, J. F. y Folguera, F., *Gaudí*. Barcelona, Editorial Sintes, 1928.

Ràfols, José F., *Gaudí*. Barcelona, Aedos, 1960.

Solà-Morales, Ignasi de, *Gaudí*. Barcelona, Polígrafa cop., 1983.

Torii,Tokutoshi, *El mundo enigmático de Gaudí*. Editorial Castalia, 1983.

Tolosa, Luis, Barcelona, *Gaudí y la Ruta del Modernismo*. Barcelona, H. Kliczkowski, 2000.

Van Zandt, Eleanor, *La vida y obras de Gaudí*. Londres, Parragon Book Service Limited, 1995.

Zerbst, Rainer. *Antoni Gaudí*. Colonia, Benedikt Taschen, 1985.

Acknowledgments

Danksagungen

We would like to express our gratitude to Daniel Giralt-Miracle, commissioner of the International Year of Gaudí, for his collaboration with the preface. To Joan Bassegoda i Nonell, of the Reial Càtedra Gaudí, for providing the drawings of most of the projects. To Gabriel Vicenç, for the invaluable information that he provided about the cathedral of Palma de Mallorca. To the Museu Comarcal Salvador Vilaseca of Reus, for one of the photographs of Antoni Gaudí. To the Arxiu Nacional de Catalunya, for the Brangulí photograph of the architect. To AZ Disseny S.L., which produces and distributes exclusive, exact reproductions of furnishings by Antoni Gaudí (tel.: 0034 932 051 581. www.cambrabcn.es/gaudi). To the Gaudí Club. And to all the photographers who collaborated on the project.

Wir bedanken uns herzlich bei Daniel Giralt-Miracle, Kommissar des Gaudí-Jahres, für seine Mitarbeit am Vorwort. Bei Joan Bassegoda i Nonell vom Königlichen Gaudí-Lehrstuhl dafür, dass er die Zeichnungen für die meisten Projekte zur Verfügung stellte. Bei Gabriel Vicenç für die unschätzbaren Informationen, die er uns zur Kathedrale von Palma de Mallorca überlassen hat. Bei dem Museu Comarcal Salvador Vilaseca von Reus für eine der Fotografien von Antoni Gaudí. Bei dem Arxiu Nacional de Catalunya für die Fotografie Brangulís von dem Architekten. Bei AZ Disseny S.L., die exklusiv die originalgetreuen Reproduktionen der Möbel von Antoni Gaudí herstellt und vertreibt (www.cambrabcn.es/gaudí). Beim Gaudí-Club sowie bei sämtlichen Fotografen, die an dem Projekt mitgearbeitet haben.

Photo credits

Fotonachweis

THE LIFE OF GAUDÍ / DAS LEBEN GAUDÍS:

36   Museu Comarcal Salvador
          Vilaseca, Reus
58   Branguli. Arxiu Nacional
          de Catalunya

CASA VICENS:
64, 65, 68, 70, 74, 75
          Roger Casas
71, 72, 73, 81, 88, 89
          Miquel Tres
76, 78, 80, 82, 83, 84, 85, 86
          Pere Planells

VILLA QUIJANO – EL CAPRICHO:
          Pere Planells

FINCA GÜELL:
120, 121, 124-127, 130-133, 138-147
          Pere Planells
128, 129, 131, 134-137
          Miquel Tres

SAGRADA FAMÍLIA:
156, 162, 164, 172-173, 176, 178 180-185
          Miquel Tres
**157, 160, 162, 166, 167, 168, 170, 171,
174, 179, 186,187**
          Pere Planells

PALAU GÜELL:
198, 199, 202-205, 212-215, 220, 224-233
          Pere Planells
206-211, 216-219, 222, 223, 234-235
          Miquel Tres

PALACIO EPISCOPAL DE ASTORGA:
**236, 237, 240, 245, 248, 249, 254, 255,
258, 259, 260, 262, 263**
          Roger Casas
246, 247, 250-254, 256, 257, 261, 263
          Miquel Tres

COL·LEGI DE LES TERESIANES:
266,267,270,272
          Roger Casas
274, 276, 282, 283
          Luis Gueilburt
275, 277-281, 284, 285, 287
          Miquel Tres

CASA DE LOS BOTINES:
**288, 289, 292, 294, 295, 296, 299-301,
306-308, 312-315**
          Roger Casas
298, 302, 303-305, 309, 310, 311, 317
          Miquel Tres

Websites of interest

Interessante Webseiten

www.barcelona-on-line.es
www.come.to/gaudi
www.cyberspain.com
www.gaudiallgaudi.com
www.gaudiclub.com
www.gaudi2002.bcn.es
www.greatbuildings.com
www.reusgaudi2002.org
www.rutamodernisme.com

Gaudí's Contemporaries

Gaudís Zeitgenossen

Hotel España

Lluís Domènech i Montaner

1903

■ Sant Pau, 9-11 Barcelona

Hotel Peninsular

Unknown architect / Architekt unbekannt

1875

Sant Pau, 34 Barcelona

Casa Figueres

Antoni Ros i Güell

1902

■ Rambla, 83 / Petxina, 1 Barcelona

Reial Acadèmia
de Ciències i Arts

Josep Domènech i Estapà

1883

■ Rambla, 115 Barcelona

Editorial Montaner i Simon

Lluís Domènech i Montaner

1885

■ Aragó, 255 Barcelona

Farolas-banco
de Pere Falqués

Pere Falqués i Urpi

1906

■ Passeig de Gràcia, Barcelona

Conservatori Municipal de Música

Antoni de Falguera i Sivilla

1916

■ Bruc, 112 Barcelona

Casa Thomas

Lluís Domènech i Montaner /
Francesc Guàrdia i Vial

1898

■ Muntaner, 293 Barcelona

Can Serra

Josep Puig i Cadafalch

1906

Rambla Catalunya, 126 Barcelona

Casa Comalat

Salvador Valeri i Pupurull

1911

■ Diagonal, 442 Barcelona

Palau del Baró de Quadras

Josep Puig i Cadafalch

1904

■ Diagonal, 373 Barcelona

Casa Macaya

Josep Puig i Cadafalch

1903

■ Passeig Sant Joan, 108 Barcelona

Museu de Zoologia

Lluís Domènech i Montaner

1888

■ Parc de la Ciutadella, Barcelona

Casa Arnús

Enric Sagnier i Vilavecchia

1903

■ Manuel Arnús, 1-31 Barcelona

Casa Pérez Samanillo

Joan J. Hervás

1909-1910

 Balmes, 169 / Diagonal, 502-504 Barcelona